THE SAVAGE
NATION

THE SAVAGE
NATION

SAVING AMERICA FROM THE LIBERAL ASSAULT
ON OUR BORDERS, LANGUAGE, AND CULTURE

MICHAEL
SAVAGE

A PLUME BOOK

PLUME
Published by the Penguin Group
Penguin Group (USA) Inc., 375 Hudson Street, New York, New York 10014, U.S.A.
Penguin Books Ltd, 80 Strand, London WC2R 0RL, England
Penguin Books Australia Ltd, 250 Camberwell Road, Camberwell, Victoria 3124, Australia
Penguin Books Canada Ltd, 10 Alcorn Avenue, Toronto, Ontario, Canada M4V 3B2
Penguin Books India (P) Ltd, 11 Community Centre, Panchsheel Park, New Delhi – 110 017, India
Penguin Books (N.Z.) Ltd, Cnr Rosedale and Airborne Roads, Albany, Auckland 1310, New Zealand
Penguin Books (South Africa) (Pty) Ltd, 24 Sturdee Avenue, Rosebank, Johannesburg 2196, South Africa

Penguin Books Ltd, Registered Offices: 80 Strand, London WC2R 0RL, England

Published by Plume, a member of Penguin Group (USA) Inc. This is an authorized reprint of
a hardcover edition published by WND Books, a division of Thomas Nelson Publishers. For
information address Thomas Nelson Publishers, Nashville, Tennessee.

First Plume Printing, March 2004
10 9 8 7 6 5 4 3 2 1

Scripture quotations noted NKJV are from THE NEW KING JAMES VERSION. Copyright
© 1979, 1980, 1982, Thomas Nelson, Inc., Publishers.

Scripture quotations noted NIV are from the HOLY BIBLE: NEW INTERNATIONAL
VERSION ®. Copyright © 1973, 1978, 1984 by International Bible Society. Used by per-
mission of Zondervan Publishing House. All rights reserved.

 REGISTERED TRADEMARK—MARCA REGISTRADA

The Library of Congress has catalogued the Thomas Nelson edition as follows:
Savage, Michael.
    The Savage nation : saving America from the liberal assault on our borders, language,
and culture / Michael Savage.
        p. cm.
    ISBN 0-7852-6353-5 (hc.)
    ISBN 0-452-28494-5 (pbk.)
    1. Liberalism—United States. 2. Social values—United States. 3. United States—Moral
conditions. 4. United States—Civilization. 5. Savage, Michael. 6. Radio broadcasters—
United States—Biography. I. Title.
    JC574.2.U6 S28 2002
    306'.0973—dc21   2002015081

Printed in the United States of America

For Janet, Becky and Russ.

We all thank Samuel and Fannie,
the astronauts of the family.

CONTENTS

~

THE SAVAGE NATION
CONTAINS ADULT LANGUAGE,
ADULT CONTENT, PSYCHOLOGICAL NUDITY

READER DISCRETION ADVISED

THE SAVAGE
NATION

1

FROM THE BRONX TO BROADCASTING

∼

Let me tell you my story before I tell you the story of the Savage Nation. Because if you think I'm just another immigrant basher, think again. I'm the son of an immigrant. I was born in New York City in an immigrant home. We had a little apartment in the Bronx. My father worked his way up from selling things in the street to having his own store. He was never wealthy, but he was never poor. He always managed to support the family.

My mother never worked. That's the way it was. My father didn't want her to. And I don't think she wanted to. But she kept that apartment clean and neat. That place was immaculate. You came in there any time of the day or night and that woman would cook three meals for anybody—they'd always be ready. And she's still kicking at eighty-seven. She's got Parkinson's, God bless that woman. You go to her house, and if she knows you're coming, to this day she'll prepare a six-course meal even though you tell her not to.

That's the background I came from. It was a very straight house, you know—a tough kind of upbringing. Life was hard in many ways, but I never missed a meal. Besides, it gave me a work ethic and values and a love for America that nobody's ever been able to take away from me.

I remember how important education was to my father. He was not an educated man. He didn't have the opportunity. Being the man-child in the promised land, I knew that the burden of my family's dreams fell on my shoulders. They felt very strongly that I should do well in school. As an immigrant's son, I don't have to tell you how hard that pressure was, since I was not a natural student.

I had to struggle to get good grades, and the reason was my mind did not focus on memorizing things. I wasn't that kind of guy. I was a dreamer, I was a philosopher, I was a thinker, but I didn't know any of that at the time. I just thought I was stupid.

Back then, the kids who could memorize were considered the bright kids. But they turned out not to be that bright. They're like the smart idiots who wound up at Harvard Law School. They became the liberal fools who can remember every law book they ever read, but they don't know what they're talking about or where they've dragged the nation.

Anyway, as I was about to enter high school, I remember my father and I drove past the high school where I was going to start the next year. It was a cold, miserable, East Coast night—the kind where it was already dark at 4:00 P.M. I remember looking at the cupola of the high school and then saying to myself, *Man, I wish I could get all A's when I go there, but I know I can't. Because I just can't, I know I can't. If I only had a magic pencil that could skip across the tests and check the right boxes, it would make my parents so proud of me.*

Today, of course, the teachers union has just about eliminated testing. They favor outcome-based "learning," which has more to do with the feelings of a student than with their grasp of knowledge.

Later on, in high school, I came home with jazz music. I became infatuated with jazz. I remember listening to Cannonball Adderley's *This Here* and my father going crazy. He said to me, "What are you listening to that junky music for? It'll warp your mind." I said, "Well, what do you want me to listen to?"

That was just the way fathers and sons were in those days. I sup-

2

pose today if a kid brought home a record from a foreign nation the father would have to be like Mr. Rogers: "Oh, son, that's just so sensitive of you. How multicultural of you, son. Have you learned much about their culture? Oh, that's so wonderful."

We didn't have room for cute in my life. Things were tough every day of our lives. And we made the best of it. Frankly, that's why I'm driven the way I am. I was raised on neglect, anger, and hate. I was raised the old-fashioned way.

Today, you raise your child with, "Oh, look at that, dear, he smeared his feces on the wall. That's modern art." Well, what are you going to produce? A journalist? You might produce a lawyer. I mean, that's about all you can make out of a kid like that. That's if he doesn't wind up with a needle in his arm and an earring on his you-know-what.

No. You've got to raise your kids tough.

I will bet a million dollars that military uniforms for children will become big, big popular toys again. I want to see kids running around with guns going, "B-b-b-b-bang, you're dead." You know, instead of putting on a dress and an earring. For ten years, kids were told to be sensitive, you know, come to school in a dress.

Not me. I grew up with a cap gun in my hand. I loved cap guns. I used to run around the streets in the Bronx shooting people in the streets with them. No one ever said, "Oh, Mrs. Savage, your son is sick. Look at that, he's aiming his gun at people and shooting it. What's wrong with him?" Every kid did that in those days. All of a sudden, the seventies came along. If you gave your kid a cap gun, you were considered psychotic. Instead, you're supposed to give him a collection of flags from the United Nations.

As poor as we were, I went on to a city college and worked a few jobs. About ten years later, I went on to get my doctorate at the University of California, Berkeley. Even then, I didn't get affirmation from my family. While education was considered important, they weren't quick to acknowledge it. It's astounding. They'd rather die of anthrax than give me the satisfaction of calling me up and saying, "Michael, you have a Ph.D. from Berkeley, you've written books on the immune system, what do you know about anthrax? What can I do to defend myself?"

Before leaving memory lane, I must tell you, one of my most cherished photos is of my paternal grandparents. I never met my grandfather; he died young. He was like the astronaut of the family to me. He's the one who left the old country, came here, worked his heart out, got the others over here, and then he dropped dead at forty-seven.

Life was hard, so we worked hard. I have no patience for the bums today whose hands are always out—you know the type. Those card-carrying "victims" who only know how to suck the nipple of Aunt Sam.

THE THEATER OF THE MIND

I should mention that one reason I love radio is that I grew up listening to radio. Unlike kids today who have a giant-screen TV set in their bedroom, I didn't grow up on television. I sat on my father's lap in our living room as he smoked Philip Morris cigarettes (I should sue the Philip Morris company because my father died too young from using their product). I can still remember his yellow, nicotine-stained fingers as I listened to *The Green Hornet*, *Inner Sanctum Mysteries*, and *The Lone Ranger*.

Of course, when I heard the Lone Ranger riding his horse, I thought there was a real horse in the radio studio. That all changed when my mother took me to the Rockefeller Center where, in the NBC Building, I saw how they generated the sound effects. I couldn't believe a man was creating the sound with fake horse hoofs. And the thunder? Just a piece of sheet metal. It was all so amazing to me as a kid.

Interestingly, not long ago, there was a study that said some of the best people in the radio business today grew up on radio. And

I think that's one reason why nobody can touch me in the sound effects department on my radio show today. I was raised on a medium that stretched my imagination.

On another level, let me tell you how I learned to communicate with an otherwise deaf and blind world. You see, I had a brother who's name was Jerome. He was born blind, largely deaf, and totally paralyzed. He lived in our little apartment with us for five or six years of his sad life. The idiot medical doctor of the neighborhood warned my mother to keep the healthy siblings away from the unhealthy. I think he thought the birth defect was catching.

I loved my brother. When I was alone with him, even though I was told he couldn't understand me, I would whistle to him in a certain way that was our secret. Guess what, Dr. Schmuck? My brother would smile, just for me. Then, when I'd hear my mother turn the key in the door of our apartment, I'd dash away.

The same doctor convinced my poor parents to send Jerome away to a state institution when he was five or six. He said it was better for the healthy children to get the sick one out of the house. For the next twenty years, once a week like clockwork, on Wednesdays I think, my mother would make the three-hour trip by bus and subway. She'd spend the day in that hellhole, taking care of Jerome. For days afterward, she could hardly speak, her face was white.

In his silence, Jerome shaped all our lives. And one day, I'll tell the whole story. Before I leave this chapter of my life, I want you to know why I so detest the Americans with Disabilities Act. It was passed to grant extra compassion for the truly needy but has been exploited by the greedy, legal profession, and those with fake handicaps who hide behind a charade to cover their laziness.

HOW I LEARNED HUMOR

I grew up in a very bad neighborhood. The kids were vicious. You could say I grew up in a *Lord of the Flies* neighborhood. That's what it was like when I was a child. In my elementary school, the bathrooms were both dangerous and rank. They smelled like a crematorium. If I went into the rest room in the first, second, or third grade in the South Bronx, I had to do my thing quickly.

I remember there was usually a bigger kid in the bathroom waiting there, leaning against the wall with a knife in his pocket. He looked to take your lunch or your money. See, back then it was grades one through eight. They didn't have anything called "middle school." In the eighth grade, you might have someone held back three years because, unlike today, you didn't automatically get moved to the next grade if you were failing. So this kid could be sixteen years old. A juvenile delinquent with a zip gun or a knife.

I'm five and he's sixteen.

I'm like 1'9" and he's 6'2".

I've gotta do my business and get out of there alive.

So, what do you do? You're a little kid, five or six years old, he's sixteen and glowering at you. To survive, I had to learn to tell quick jokes. I would disarm the guy with humor. I prepare to take care of my business, and while I'm doing it, I'm disarming him with a story with my hand in the air and mesmerizing him like a snake charmer.

I would say, "Listen, wait a minute, hold on, I want to tell you blah, blah, blah." He'd stand there waiting for the punch line. By the time I finagled him, I was finished, zipped up, and out. And that's the truth.

That's how I learned humor. Admittedly, talk radio is not quite as demanding as relieving oneself in a Bronx bathroom.

I always had the gift of making people laugh. You know, I don't mind if people say I'm a great entertainer. That's a great compliment. That used to bother me. People used to be able to get under my skin when they'd say, "I don't believe a word you say, but you really make me laugh. You're very entertaining." Fine, I used to get angry.

But, I can't be funny every day; let's start with that. So much of what I see happening to America makes me mad. People say, "Oh, you know, Savage, when you get angry the women don't listen to your show. They get scared and they hang up. They tune in to something else. Stick to the humor."

It's probably true. Women are afraid of angry men. Particularly in this homosexualized, feminized America. An angry man frightens a woman. If a boyfriend can't be like a girlfriend (with the exception of a male appendage), she doesn't want him. If a boyfriend can't be like a sister putting on nails with her, she's offended by him. If a boyfriend doesn't look like an emaciated model on heroin, she's afraid of him.

So, what can I do? That's the way I am. My vocal cords are what they are. And the fact of the matter is, so is my testosterone level, and so is my anger and rage level. And, no, I don't plan to go to anger management classes in the very near future. I'll let God take care of that at the end of the road. Anger management comes when they put me in the ground. That's when the anger management starts. In the next world. I don't want to manage it in this world.

You manage your anger, Mr. Liberal, because that's another one of your liberal tricks. You find the man who gets furious and really wants to change things. You tell him he's a psychotic and he needs anger management. You know what I say? "Drop dead." That's what I say. I've said it since the first day. Don't try to manage me or my anger. It's not your business.

You know how all this anger management started? It started with women when I was very young. They'd say to me, "Michael, you're not being a gentleman," when I would do something that offended them. And I'd say, "You know what? I'm not a gentleman. I'm a man. So you can take the 'gentle' out of it. And you'll find out that you can trust me more than you can your 'gentleman' friends who put a knife in your back at the first opportunity."

Humor is powerful. And humor can be great if it's used for a purpose. Most comedians are not funny, if you've ever analyzed them.

Good comedy is social commentary. It's not stupid comedy-club lines like, "I was putting the Clairol on my head. And you know, it ran down on my face, and it looked like my Aunt Gertie. Ha, ha, ha." You know the kind of stuff you see at a comedy workshop, where they talk about bodily functions—that's not comedy. That's just stupid vaudeville. That's what passes for humor and comedy.

Comedy is what I sometimes do. Comedy is social satire. That's what comedy should be. That's what it was invented for. That's what God gave me the gift for. So, when I can, I use it. Some days I can't.

THE SAVAGE STORY

In the history of the human mind, there's never been a profession like radio. Never. There's nothing to match it. I grew up believing that the novelist was the epitome of the intellectual. But in time I came to believe scientists had the greatest minds. I wanted to be a scientist, and so I trained in the field and became a scientist. But then I found out that scientists' minds are very much run-of-the-mill minds in our time.

By the time I had arrived at the university level, most of the great minds were gone. You had more academic businessmen. There's nothing wrong with being an academic businessman. But I quickly learned science was very much a business. If you wanted to get ahead, you had to get grants. To get grants, you had to do pedestrian scientific studies and appeal to the idiots in Washington who granted the money. And, so, I found there was very little groundbreaking science being produced anymore.

It was then I discovered there was something new out there called talk radio. Tell me when in history you can take a human being who (1) has the ability and gift to project his ideas, (2) does his homework and knows how to convey those ideas, and (3) attracts people every day to listen to him and call him. There's never been anything like it.

At the time, I was writing books. One of my publishers was

Houghton-Mifflin in Boston. The book was *Maximum Immunity*, which sold sixty thousand hardcover copies. So, don't assume for a minute that they were junk books and marginally published. They weren't. They were top of the line. They were the Rolls-Royce of the field.

I had a wonderful editor, who will remain anonymous. I remember she once said to me over lunch at a fancy chowder house in Boston, "Michael, as I've gotten to know you, I think you ought to go into radio." I'm talking 1983 when there really was no big thing in talk radio. There were a couple of guys around, but it wasn't what it is today.

When I asked her why radio, she said, "Because you like immediate feedback. Think of it. You think of a book, then you have to sell the book idea to a publisher, then you have to get a contract, then you gotta write the book. By the time the book comes out, your mind is somewhere else. It's three, four years later." She was right, but I didn't act on her suggestion immediately; the idea seemed too unbelievable to me.

Funny thing, every time I did a book tour, I'd come back home and meet some honest people in radio. They told me the same thing as my editor. They'd say, "You know, you have a great voice and you think quick on your feet, which makes for great radio. Your insights are better than anyone's out there. You ought to consider a radio show." I said, "Thanks for the compliment—but how do I get into that field? I'm an author. How am I ever going to get into radio?"

Now, if I were a liberal, I would have applied for a grant from the National Endowment for the Arts and demanded a government-subsidized handout. Not me. I decided to make a radio demo, fake callers and all. I sent it to 250 radio stations. Five called and offered me a job on the spot. One of those stations was in San Francisco. I got hired to do fill-ins, weekends, and the graveyard shifts. Fine. It was a start.

But when you're good, you're good. When my show broke new ground in the ratings, I was handed an offer I couldn't refuse. And here we are. The Savage Nation is the fastest-growing syndicated radio talk show in the country.

And do you know what my greatest pleasure is every day on my show? I love the taste of liberals in the afternoon and evening. They're particularly succulent by the end of the day. It's something that you gotta understand is better than Kentucky Fried Chicken for me.

WINNERS AND LOSERS

I, having come from these humble beginnings, am where I am today because of two words: *attitude* and *gratitude*. I'll explain.

I went to have dinner—I'm not gonna name the restaurant—but it was on Fisherman's Wharf, my favorite seafood/Italian restaurant. I was sitting there looking at the fishing boats, enjoying a glass of wine, and waiting for the calamari and this and that. A waiter came over to me, really nice guy. He happened to be of African-American descent. I have to mention that for a reason you'll see as the story evolves.

"Mr. Savage," he said, "I just want to say that my mother and my grandmother have listened to your show for years. They were the ones who introduced me to your show." As we talked, I was impressed by his positive attitude. Not for one second did I sense he carried a chip on his shoulder—he never once blamed me for the oppression of black people two hundred years ago.

After listening to him for a few minutes, I said, "I'll bet you were raised to believe in America, to believe in the value of hard work, and I'll bet you're a churchgoing man." He couldn't agree more. As he left the table, he said to me with a smile, "Mr. Savage, keep on testifying."

See, I wanted him to understand something. He was successful in life because of the attitude that his mother and grandmother put into his mind. Many people who come from humble backgrounds end up with the wrong ideas in their head. It's easy to go wrong in the world if you let demagogues like Al Sharpton, Jesse Hijackson, or Tom Daschle sell you the victimology mentality.

I see it all the time. Unlike my waiter, if you think the government owes you an entitlement, you wind up hating the world. Then you think *everyone* owes you a living, and so you walk around with your hand out. When you don't get what you want, you wind up believing everyone is your enemy.

And you know what else you end up with?

A big fat zero in life.

My waiter didn't get that warped view because he had a strong set of values instilled by his mother and grandmother who took the time to teach him the right way. I should mention this young man works in one of the most upscale restaurants in the city. He's doing great. He works where the tips are high. And believe me, being a waiter in an upscale restaurant is a good job for many people.

How did he get there? He certainly didn't get there by accident. As you well know, even in the table-waiting field there are gradations. He got the job in this fine restaurant because his attitude was right and he wasn't afraid of hard work.

That's what's so wrong with the liberal entitlement message passed down in our society. Just sit on your fat behind, watch TV, swill another drink, and be sure to wait for your welfare check on Friday.

One other point on winners and losers:

I had a show where a number of eighty-year-olds called in. Let me just say every one of them was cheerful and positive. They were uplifting. You have to respect that in a person. Somehow along the way I learned in order to survive, I've got to be positive about life. Being positive and hopeful is so hard to remember in a society that's so negative.

On the other hand, there's a common denominator among the losers that I've met in my life. You know what that is? Their inability to give the other man credit for anything.

As a teenager, I had the same mentality—that no matter what anyone around you may have achieved or accomplished, you ran them down. You never gave the other man any credit. I never thought that by doing so, you'd be digging your own grave.

But I've since learned to think differently. I have found that successful people, particularly those who made it on their own, have a respect for other people. In other words, when they know somebody did something that's worthy of respect, they give it to that person. I've met people worth hundreds of millions of dollars who still know how to give the next man respect for his or her achievements. They refuse to sit there and run the other guy down—unlike the losers, who run everyone down. They are like latrine slime, always on the bottom.

I knew one such guy. He lived in a rat hole in this city, a real hater of humanity. All he did was talk about his World War II experience on a boat and how the whole world owed him a living. He made it clear nobody was any good, everybody was wrong, and he was quick to blame his problems on one ethnic group or another.

This loser didn't know how to say "thank you" to anybody. As a matter of fact, I saved him from cancer. He was given up for dead in a VA hospital with a tumor under his arm the size of a grapefruit. More than twelve years ago I put him on a special nutrition program, and he was cured of that cancer.

And you know what? That guy never said "thank you" to me. Twelve years later, after being sent home from a VA hospital to die, he's alive. And yet this loser, the most unsuccessful man I ever met in my life, never said thank you to Michael Savage for saving his life.

What I'm trying to tell you is that success in life is all about attitude and gratitude.

THE MUGGER AND THE BEATNIK POET

When I finish a show, many nights I like to go for a walk. I'll never forget this particular beautiful evening. The cool air felt good on my face. I had a knit cap on, a pea coat. I was just walking in the streets of San Francisco enjoying life, looking at the people. I noticed two couples in the crosswalk in front of me.

Behind them was a street bum, one of the plagues of America, drunk, whacked out of his mind on crack. I watched and listened as he insulted the girl: "I'd sure like to get her; I like the one with the black hair, I want her." You know, one of *those* guys—nice fellow.

It wasn't my business so I stayed away from it. I don't blame the boys who were walking with the girls for not saying anything because this bum was an animal that should be in a cage, not on the street, as you will soon hear.

Incidentally, San Francisco is filled with a human plague like this because of the ultraliberalism that is killing the city. I'm convinced it's the only city left in America that permits eels like this to crawl around, bothering everybody, and assaulting the women verbally. Every other city has cracked down on them, but not this city. It's the city of, well, not tolerance, but of hatred.

Hatred for anything normal.

Hatred for law and order.

Hatred for decency.

Hatred for mama and apple pie and the roses in your hand.

Just as we were crossing the crosswalk, a cab tried to cut us off and almost killed six of us. I naturally turned around and screamed at the driver, "Go back to where you came from," and that type of thing. He was a swarthy Middle Easterner, but I couldn't have cared less.

Now, the guy next to me, the bum, turns and says, "Well, don't worry, if he hits the five, I give him nine." He pulled out a 9mm gun. Remember, this guy is cracked out of his mind. He's drunk, and he's waving the gun around. And I'm thinking, *Okay, quick situation*

13

check here: This guy is volatile. I'm white, he's black, he's out of his mind. He's looking for somebody, but it ain't gonna be me. So I said to him, "Hey man, put the gun away. The cops will get you."

Suddenly we became, for that instant, coconspirators. He said to me, "Yeah, right, I shouldn't do it. But if that cab got to me, I'd put nine into him."

I want you to understand the meaning of this story. The streets are crawling with crazy people with guns in their hands. The gun grabbers *should* take the guns away from the psychopaths. But instead, the Dianne Feinsteins of the world, the Charlie Schumers, the subway senators, they want to take the guns away from the middle class, leaving us completely defenseless while they remain protected by the Secret Service.

This is just another reason liberalism, like a backed-up toilet, offends me. Libs turn common sense into no-sense. When ultraliberalism takes over the mind of a city, streets are no longer safe, people are defenseless, and wackos with weapons get free handouts.

Later that evening I walked up the street and passed San Francisco's once-famous communist bookstore. Low and behold, God had answered my prayers. In the window, there was a memorial to a human eel. Part mortadella salami, part latrine slime. I won't mention his name because he's insignificant, and you've never heard of him.

He was a junkie, an alcoholic, and had babies like dogs do, never raised any of them, just impregnated women. And, of course, he was loved by the left wing because he was one of the last reigning beatnik poets.

Anyway, there was a picture of him in the window of this commie bookstore. Next to his photo was a letter to the mayor of the city, asking for some proclamation for the so-called poet who had died. It said, "We want to proclaim that this day forward is a day of memorial for latrine slime mortadella."

I clasped my hands together and prayed to God. I said, "Thank you, God, for answering my prayers. One of the blights of the human race is gone." As I said that to myself in front of this store on the streets of San Francisco, a couple of tourists were going by. One of them smiled and said, "Ooh, who's latrine slime?" I said, "Just about anybody that the owner of this communist bookstore cares to put in his window," and I walked on.

Can you blame me for rejoicing? The damage these ultraliberals are doing to the country I inherited is inexcusable. Frankly, my evening got better from that point on, once I realized that the mortadella human had crossed the River Styx.

I hated him. I hated his guts.

SAVAGE MEATBALL LETTER

One of the joys of hosting the Savage Nation is the incredible e-mail I get. I get thousands of pieces of e-mail a week. I read most of them, some of them others screen. This particular afternoon, I was eating a Chinese lunch while reading a huge stack of e-mail.

By the way, when they served my meal, I remembered why I hadn't eaten chicken curry in years. I know they use rendered fat in Chinese restaurants. That stuff is beyond anything you can imagine. The brown gravy they used on this chicken curry, it's like Drano wouldn't dissolve it. You have to go back to high school chemistry with pure sulfuric acid to cut it. That's the kind of gravy it was. I'm trying to avoid it; I know it's clogging my arteries. But I ate it anyway because it was Friday.

So, I'm opening the mail, and I come to a letter. It said, "Dear Michael, I'm gonna hereby end all the meatball talk, because I make the best Italian-American meatballs, period. And that's all there is to it."

I read on because anyone who says that right off the bat has more to say than meatballs, and I knew it was coming. It was a five-page letter.

He said, "I make the best meatballs, and here's how it's done." The guy actually gave me a recipe. Naturally, I'm not gonna give it to you.

He wrote, "That's all there is to meatballs. Sooner or later you're gonna want to graduate to the next level of meatball consciousness. I make a meatball sandwich in the creation of which I am known as the world's expert."

I love this. Guts. The guy said, "The thing about a meatball sandwich to keep in mind is that the meatballs are the star. You don't want to get distracted by the sauce, bread, or cheese. So nothing fancy."

Now listen to how specific this guy is. He said, "Choose a French roll that's a little soft and less crusty than you'd use for a regular deli sandwich. No sourdough—I hate sourdough. That's a California thing. It's supposed to be good. I never liked it. You want bread that can suck up the juice."

As you can imagine, I'm eating this up. Even his words are rich. This is a Mark Twain letter. "Slice the roll down the side, but not all the way to the ends. Or, cut off one end and hollow out the middle, almost like a pita. Use a sauce that's thinner than spaghetti or pizza sauce. You want it to soak into the bread. You put on some sauce, then meatballs."

Right about now, I lost my interest in the chicken curry. He said, "Use a good melting cheese like mozzarella that will get stringy like pizza cheese." And he underlines, "no strong grated cheese like Parmesan. Remember, the meatballs rule and not the strong cheese flavor. Heat it, bake it, whatever, till it's hot and the cheese is melted. Eat it with your hands. Prepare to get it all over yourself and everything nearby." Now that's a man after my own heart.

There's not a shirt in my closet that isn't ruined from food. No matter how hard I try. It's a family joke: whatever I eat, it's on my clothes. I can't help it. I put a napkin here, it goes there. I put it there, and it squirts in my ear.

He said, "I think it goes best with a salad, maybe some large steak fries, red wine or beer if it's a hot day." Then he goes on to the best commercial place to get a meatball sandwich.

Now you're not gonna believe where he goes with this. He said, "One more thing, Savage. I'm about your age, and I grew up in the New York area. And when I was a kid/teenager I cut my eyeteeth on the consciousness-of-life area, like many a kid, by staying up secretly and listening to Gene Shepherd.

"It wasn't so much his stories or his monologues, but his ability to awaken in his listeners an awareness of the absurdities of life—of the treasure that is existence—and that a person's journey through life, whether successful or tragic, was worth every day. He made me want to live life with humor, without fear, with the ability to revere the good and laugh at myself and society's sacred cows."

I remember Gene Shepherd, and he's right. He concluded his letter this way: "Since those days, Savage, you are the only other radio personality that has been able to evoke and inspire any of that. It's just what you do best. Politics aside, I only started to listen to you every day since the election last year. Because I basically don't like to listen to call-in talk shows, but you're the best. Keep it up, and I'll keep listening."

This is the best letter I've ever gotten in my radio career. Why? Reading that one letter I got a wonderful compliment, I got a killer meatball recipe, and he got me thinking. He sparked something in my mind that goes beyond experiencing the best meatball sandwich in the world.

You see, meatballs can tell us a lot about a society.

Back when America was still moral and whole, our meatballs were big, soft, and tasty. Today, thanks mainly to the Demoncats, the libs, and the Commu-Nazis who rule the courts, America's meatballs are small, hard, and tasteless. In other words, we have replicated the Swedish meatball, which is what socialism brings.

2

DIVERSITY IS PERVERSITY

～

THE FUTURE OF AMERICA hangs in the balance like a loose tooth.
Everything you and I have worked for is being wiped out before
our eyes. Our borders, our language, and our culture are under
siege. Contrary to what you've been programmed to think by politicians with TelePrompTers, the al-Qaida network is not America's
most dangerous enemy.

Did you get that? I'll put it another way.

To fight only the al-Qaida scum is to miss the terrorist network
operating within our own borders. Who are these traitors? Every rotten, radical left-winger in this country, that's who. For years, these
empty skirts have been waging a personal war against the American
people. They smile for the cameras as they spew their phony message of tolerance, diversity, and perversity. But behind closed doors,
they line their pockets and advance their personal fortunes at our
expense.

Liberalism is unraveling the very fabric of this great nation. And
the sooner you understand that liberalism is a dangerous mental disorder, the sooner you can break free from this insanity that attacks
the way you live, how you conduct your business, the way you worship, the choice of SUV you drive, the food you eat, and the very freedoms you enjoy.

I'll show you where all this asinine liberal ideology is coming from, what it's doing to America, and where it's taking us as a country unless you and I stop it.

In the meantime, here's a perfect example of how radical liberal socialist thinking is dangerous. I give you one group of psychopaths from PETA, People for the Ethical Treatment of Animals.

The other day I heard a PETA spokeschick on the radio babbling on and on about the need for "compassionate and humane alternatives" to chicken sandwiches. I'm not making this up. Her name is unimportant. She claimed that every chicken killed for a chicken sandwich has "her throat slit" when the majority of these animals are fully conscious.

Let's stop there. The chicken has *her* throat slit?

Listen to what this lunatic is saying. She and her human-hating buddies clucked over how we process chickens, but they show little concern for the flight attendants who had their throats cut by Arab and Middle Eastern hijackers. No such sanctimony came from the mouths of these psycho nutcases with green hair and nipple rings. No. They're only concerned about a chicken having its throat cut.

Obviously, they've watched the movie *Chicken Run* one time too many. These people are lunatics. But wait, there's more.

Ms. PETA-Brain rambled on about the "hideous living conditions" of the animals and the "suffering" they experience during transportation to the slaughterhouse. What a surprise that she never expresses concern for the hideous living conditions of child slaves in China.

Can't you see what these left-wing wackos have done? They've successfully taken our minds off the real *human* suffering—both here and abroad.

They never talk about the slavery of Christians in the Sudan by Muslims. They never talk about the Chinese slaves in China. They never talk about the oppression of the Cuban people by Fidel Castro.

Instead, they hijack the entire conscience of America with absurd nonissues and then make you feel guilty for eating a McChicken sandwich.

Well, forget that. I'm going to KFC for lunch.

This clucking capon and her psychopathic cousins who have dominated the public consciousness for ten years want us to pay attention to this drivel. Why? So we forget the real excesses of the dictators running Iraq, Cuba, and North Korea, not to mention the would-be commissars in our midst. These are the human rights abuses we should focus on. Not chicken sandwiches.

That's the ignorance of liberalism, and I expose it every day. I'm not catering to these nut bars. I don't care how they may try to intimidate me. I refuse to cave in to their way of thinking. They're never going to break me.

Maybe you think this is a joke. In fact, they're hoping you do. But, as you'll see, the left-wing agenda espoused by PETA, like all radical liberal groups, is morally bankrupt at its core. Don't say I didn't warn you.

They will open this country up to further terrorism.

They will pollute everything that you believe in.

They will trample on your church.

They will trample on your synagogue.

They will trample on your flag.

They will trample on your memory.

They'll trample on your collective memory.

They'll pervert your child's mind.

They are dangerous. They're not laughable. It's people like these who brought down governments in the past.

So, let it be known I'm declaring war on liberal terrorism. Not halfway—all the way. That means right here, right now. Why? Because I hate what these bums—the wacko left-wing maniacs, the Ninth Jerk-it Court of Schlemiels, and the illiberal politicians, those pieces of dried beef in suits—are doing to America the Beautiful.

I hate the way they attack marriage and the family. I hate the way they stick their sticky fingers into my paycheck and force me to pay for some failed social program in the name of compassion. I hate their unrelenting celebration of sodomy in the midst of an AIDS epidemic, which, by the way, has largely decimated both America's blood supply and the health care industry.

And another thing. Don't bother me with your Hate-Free Zone pabulum. Every time I see a sign proclaiming an area a "Hate-Free Zone," I get hateful. I want to strangle somebody. Who are they to tell me it's a Hate-Free Zone? What if I want to hate? It's my constitutional right to hate you if you're a lowlife.

To hate you if you rape children.

To hate you if you step on the flag.

To hate you if you're a drug dealer.

To hate you if you break the crosses off war memorials.

I'm allowed to hate you. I'm not allowed to *hurt* you, but I'm allowed to hate you. What do you mean, "Hate-Free Zone"? Where'd that come from? Who invented that garbage? That's modern fascism.

That's why in the pages ahead I'll give you a "Who's Who" of social terrorism. No infospeak. No happy horse "analysis" by leg-crossers in heavy makeup. And I promise to use small words for those who can't finish reading a complete sentence without taking a hydration break.

I'll start with the left-wing pinko vermin in high places who, along with their arrogant accomplices in the media, are killing us with the twisted, mind-numbing message of ultratolerance.

Unlike what you may have heard from Dan "Blabber" or Larry "Seltzer," I'm here to tell you America's borders are overflowing with the flotsam and jetsam of humanity. Many in dirty nightshirts fabricate lies, sneak, cheat, and bribe their way into this great country only to turn around and stab us in the back with our own airplanes.

As for the clipped-haired, mean-faced Demoncats who tell me I'm hateful and intolerant because I oppose the tidal wave of Turd World immigration, I say, *Go find another country*. Who are you to judge me? You may think unlawful immigrants sucking the nipple of taxpayer subsidized healthcare is a good thing, but you're wrong, and I'll prove it.

And another thing. Why should I work sixty hours a week and then be forced by Hillary Clinton and her party of social engineers to pay for the bum class? All day long, these couch-warming leeches sit in front of their TVs, hog down soda and beer, smoke cigarettes purchased with welfare-padded wallets, and then have the nerve to whine when some brave soul in Congress suggests they be required to at least do a few hours of community service in exchange for their "entitlements."

I refuse to whistle Dixie while my country is being overrun by psycho-lib Commu-Nazi organizations like the ACLU who defend child molesters and terrorists, who trash our traditions, and who silence religious speech while wrapping themselves in the flag to justify child pornography—virtual or otherwise.

And another thing: I don't need a TelePrompTer to know what to think. In spite of what the liberal media would have me believe, and, in spite of the damage they've done to our country, everywhere I look, I'm finding evidence that America may be on the verge of a revival. I'm seeing the first signs that the old guard of liberalism is dying.

How can I tell? The American sheeple are slowly coming to their senses. They're beginning to see I was right eight years ago when I called for the tightening of our borders. Now they're demanding that we revamp our immigration policies. They're starting to understand that an "English Only" policy—English as the official language of our nation—is the glue that will hold us together. Even our patriotism has reached new levels not seen in decades.

What's more, under the Al Goreleone and Bill Clinton regime, we saw all branches of the military suffer low morale and neglect. That's changing, thank God.

Maybe your mind is awakening to politics, too. Maybe you want to join the fight to save our soil. Good. It's about time you realized how your mind has been drugged in order to make you surrender. I say it's time to snap out of the deep sleep that holds the rest of the Leno-Letterman crowd in a comatose state.

For starters, look around you, wherever you are in America. Look at the greatness of your civilization. Look at the bridges. Look at the buildings. Look at the airplanes. Look at the tele-communications, the highways, the hospitals, schools, food ser-vices, and our food production. These industries and inventions have come from your civilization. In spite of what the left may have you believe, we are blessed to be the greatest country in the history of the world.

Now, look at nations where terrorists are bred. Look how they live. Look what they've given the world. Centuries of bloodshed. Hatred. Sexism. Religious intolerance. Everything that the Enlightenment stood for, these guys in dirty nightshirts stand against.

Not me. I want to survive. I want my children to have a nation even better than the one I inherited. Yes, that's why I'm fighting for the future of America. And that's why I created the Paul Revere Society (to learn more about our efforts, visit *www.MichaelSavage.com*).

So, if you're tired of being attacked in school whenever you celebrate the achievements of America; if you're weary of being trampled on whenever you speak in favor of morality; if, as a Boy Scout, you've become a pariah while the perverts have become the victims, you've come to the right place.

You see, the book you're holding has the power to unravel years of liberal brainwashing. It has the unmatched insight and the unrestrained truth to prevent the continuous social disintegration caused by those who care only to secure the next vote through selling our interests to foreign enemies.

When it's all said and done, when you've worked your way to the last page, you will have learned that in so many cases "diversity is perversity." I'm also convinced you'll get down on your hands and knees and say, "Thank you, God; this is the only man in the country saying it the way it really is."

3

AMERICA:

From the Melting Pot to the Chamber Pot

~

I SPEAK TO FIVE MILLION Savages and Savagettes a week. They count on me for the truth. The worst attacks on Western civilization await me every day. This is my morning. T-shirt, dog, black coffee. The TV screams at me. E-mail news awaits its turn to make my day. Scanning the news of the "whorled" is what I do.

This day offends me more than most days. I stare at the pages of the "*Old York Times*" wondering what new game the liberal terrorists, with the aid of the government-media complex, are inflicting on us. Every time I read the paper, I have to decode. I'm sickened by watching the politicians, the femi-fascists, the Commu-Nazis, and the RDDBs rip apart the land I inherited.

Many of you have heard the phrase "Red Diaper Baby." I didn't invent it. I grew up hearing it. In a way, it's a laughable phrase. Then again, it's not so funny when you think what the lawyers from NYU and Columbia are doing to the country.

Years ago, we knew a "Red Diaper Baby" was someone who was raised by parents who were Communists. These parents had sympathy for Joseph Stalin, Lenin, Marx, or Engels. Take your choice of the early Bolsheviks or Commie theorists. The parents, mainly from New York, worked hard to instill in their children the Communist ideology during their formative years. As such, the children were called "Red Diaper Babies."

Over the years, I tried to understand what had happened to a plain Communist to make them literally psychotic. Here's what I discovered. When you took a child like that during the sixties and you added marijuana, it sowed the seeds of the psychosis that most of these radicals are clearly exhibiting today.

So, I renamed them: "Red Diaper *Doper* Babies"—or RDDBs.

Whether you are aware of it or not, there is a battle going on in America at all levels. In government, in education, in the courts, and in our neighborhoods. America is in the midst of a cultural crisis.

I realize my observations may be painful to you, especially if you are a product of today's socialist-run, education-media system. During the Vietnam War, schools stopped teaching American history in favor of lessons in white male crimes for ancient wrongdoings. Educators traded in their history books in favor of *Tommy Has Two Mommies*.

You were never taught basic American history.

America was founded as a nation of law and order, of checks and balances. We were to be governed by the Constitution, not by a king. Three branches of government were created: the executive, the judicial, and the legislative. Each branch of government served to balance the power so that America didn't end up with a dictator like "Sodom" Hussein running the place. Our government was designed to operate "for the people, by the people."

That's why Americans enjoy religious freedom.

Americans enjoy the right to own property.

Americans enjoy the right to bear arms.

Americans have freedom of speech.

You even have a right to be an American moron. Just look at the Hollywood idiots. These rights are what set us apart from the rest of the world. They're a part of the American identity, and the freedom these rights ensure have allowed creative, enterprising minds to find the cure to various diseases, to improve our health care system, to maximize our quality of life, and to send a man to the moon.

But, if the left-wingers who control what is broadcast, the press, and the entertainment industries are to be believed, America is to be blamed for the pollution of the planet and the destruction of the ozone layer. According to the left, we're responsible for all human suffering and oppression. And, no matter how far we bend over backward to accommodate lefty activists, we're accused of discrimination and assorted hate crimes. Even Rat Boy's decision to join the Taliban is somehow our fault.

So I sat back in my chair and forced myself to consider: What makes these freedoms so special? Why are we the envy of the entire world? Why should I bother to fight the Red Diaper Doper Babies of the ACLU and their radical liberal socialist buddies when they ambush the Constitution and assault the American Dream?

In other words I, as a conservative, had to ask myself, *Is America still worth fighting for?*

Before I give you my answer, what about you? Are America and the Bill of Rights worth defending? Do you care about the invasion of our borders, our language, and our culture by those who would happily sling dung at the principles on which America was founded?

Maybe you can't answer the question because you're not sure if you're a lib or a conservative. Let me make it easy for you. Are you ready for this?

You can tell your political orientation based upon how you reacted to the 9/11 attack on America. Keep in mind that what Hitler couldn't do, what Tojo couldn't do, these pirates in filthy nightshirts achieved by bringing down two of our greatest buildings. And why did they attack America?

Because they are hateful.

They are jealous.

They are destructive.

They create nothing. And, for the past seven hundred years their only contribution to world history has been death, oppression, fear, bondage, and terror.

So how did you react to the news that America was assaulted?

Liberals, while the Twin Towers were still a fresh smoldering pile of body parts and rubble, rushed to *understand* our enemies. They bought books on Islam. They wanted to determine if maybe, just maybe, we did something to provoke the attack.

In other words, a liberal is someone who wants to understand the guy who just broke into his house, who burned the place down, who raped his wife and who murdered his kids. Yes, the liberal wants to discover what he or she might have done wrong to *deserve* the attack.

The conservative doesn't care what religious affiliation the villain hides behind, what holy robes he may wear, or what he calls himself. When he sees the enemy coming to rape his wife and kill his children, the conservative shoots him dead before he gets *in* the house. He doesn't wring his hands and get a book out to study the belief system of the murderer.

I'm telling you, this lunacy has got to stop.

In 1776, Thomas Paine said, "What we obtain too cheap, we esteem too lightly; it is dearness only that gives everything its value." Your problem is that you've been handed everything on a silver platter. The truth is, you don't know how good you've got it in America. This may help: There is only *one* country in the world that attracts people from virtually every other country.

Don't you get it? Everybody wants what *you* have.

About half the world goes to bed listening to the sound of their empty, bloated stomachs grumbling. They have no doctors. No dentists. No paved roads. No houses. No clothing. No hope. And, if they dare speak against the thugs who hold their country hostage, they win a quick trip to the death camps where their organs can be harvested (as in China). The leftists or liberals, of course, would have you believe these depredations are *our* fault. The fault of the evil white male.

I believe America, the land of the free and the home of the brave, is worth fighting for—and no dirty liberal traitor can change my mind about that. So, having determined to press on, I reached for the e-mails, poured another cup of coffee, and hoped for the best.

That's when I came across a story that really got my blood boiling. We Americans are losing basic freedoms to the freaks who would enslave us with sensitivity classes.

BARNEY:
THE LIBS' IDEA OF A PURPLE HEART

Let me tell you about Richard Oulton. But beware. If you have even an ounce of red, white, and blue blood left running through your veins, this story could cause you to bust a major artery. I can't think of a better example to demonstrate that America is becoming the land of the freaks and the home of the slaves—thanks to the mental disease of liberalism.

According to the report, Richard was given a Purple Heart, which, for you Lexus Liberals, is a military honor given to members of the armed forces who spilled their blood defending their country. Richard served on the front lines as a member of the "Walking Dead Marines" of the First Battalion, Ninth Marine Regiment. They started with eight hundred marines in the battalion. Six hundred and five were mowed down in action. Richard's unit suffered the highest casualties of any unit in the Vietnam War.

Years later, Richard and his family retired in an upscale community in Richmond, Virginia. When I say upscale, we're talking big houses, manicured lawns, the picture of the American Dream. Fine. I say, God bless him. According to the story, on Memorial Day, 1999, Richard proudly flew the American flag and the Purple Heart flag atop a flagpole outside his home.

And why not? This is America the last time I checked.

The next day, a member of the Wyndham Property Owners Association, which governs his community with all the finesse of the Hitler Brigade, informed Richard the flags he flew were a "visual nuisance." He was informed he must remove the "eyesore" or face charges. How could he be so *insensitive* as to raise a flag on Memorial Day?

But wait. After serving papers to ban the flag display on his private property, an employee of H. H. Hunt, the developer of the Wyndham community, went on the radio to discuss the action. Ms. Kim Beard boasted that they had previously ordered a Purple Barney statue removed from another homeowner's lawn. The implication was clear: There's no fundamental difference between a purple Barney and a Purple Heart.

Take down the American flag? The Purple Heart flag a nuisance? I'll tell you where you can put that flagpole, you moron.

It gets more unbelievable. When Richard Oulton refused, the association took him to court. Never mind the fact that all the adjoining neighbors signed a petition *in favor* of the flag display. Never mind the fact that nowhere in the association's 150 pages of restrictions, covenants, and guidelines did it prohibit the display of flags on a flagpole.

So, off to court we go.

How did the Dishonorable L. A. Harris, a modern liberal Commu-Nazi judicial benchwarmer, handle the American flag, which his forefathers (probably buried in the rubble under his courthouse) died to protect? Judge Harris awarded the Wyndham Association $87,585.58 in damages, citing the concern that the display of the flag could lower property values.

Damages? What, for their *feelings* being hurt?

See, that's exactly how liberalism works. Punish the people who shed their blood to protect your rights. But the asininity doesn't end there. Harris the harebrain ordered the flag be forever lowered and then required the Oulton family to post an additional $95,000 bond or forfeit the opportunity to an appeal. This public servant had to drain his retirement savings in order to fight for his right to fly a flag.

You see, sheeple, there's a fascinating aspect of this freak show I haven't told you about. The city of Richmond, home to this insanity, is the very city where Patrick Henry stated his famous call to arms during the Second Virginia Convention: "Give me liberty or give me death!" The men and women in Patrick Henry's day paid the ultimate price to break free from the tyranny of the British Empire. Now, thanks to left-wing commissars and their sensitivity police, Richard Oulton's gated community has more in common with a police state than with the freedom of America.

And so, I must confront this liberal lunacy with the words of our sixth president, John Quincy Adams, in hopes that a bell of clear thinking will echo inside your head as you read it:

> Posterity—you will never know how much it has cost my genera-
> tion to preserve your freedom. I hope you will make good use of it.

THE WHITE HOUSE SHOULD BE BLACK

Do you have any idea where all this sensitivity nonsense is taking us? I'll tell you. I predict the day is coming when the Reverend Jesse Hijackson or some such subversive minority group will insist it's time to change the White House to the Multi-Culty House.

I can already imagine what their childish, whiney protest would sound like. They'd argue the White House symbolizes the power of white males. I can picture the Reverend Hijackson standing on Pennsylvania Avenue with the White House in the background. He'd say, "It's time to end it. Not mend it." He'd suggest the White House should be painted black or brown and renamed the Black House or the Brown House. Don't we sheeple know it's racist to have to call it the White House?

But in the land of the freaks and slaves, they won't stop there. No, my friend. They'll tell us white paint should be illegal in America. Of course, they'd start on a voluntary basis. But any paint store that sold white would be picketed and any manufacturer of white paint would be signaling they're white supremacists. Anyone who makes white paint would be sued.

You think I'm kidding? These are the same people who equate a Purple Heart with Barney.

These illegitimate phonies would go a step further and make the color white illegal. Anyone who uses white paper would be branded a racist. Why would we permit children to use white paper in schools when paper comes in yellow, pink, and gray? These mental cases are going to accuse us of demonstrating, symbolically of course, that the white is superior. They'll say we're attempting to brainwash impressionable young minds with a message of hate.

Now, of course, in the new whorled order ushered in by liberalism, we'd have to change the color of clouds in time. I'm sure that with proper chemistry applied to this important problem, we could change the clouds to black clouds or brown clouds. Because those white clouds, unto themselves, are probably offensive to people of color. They represent clean, pure whiteness—absolutely an elitist concept that must be eliminated immediately.

Just wait. Senator Hillary Clinton, in an attempt to secure the minority vote, will suggest we take the money Bush is going to waste on the missile defense shield and turn it into a grant to fund those who could find a way to color the clouds black or brown, thereby making the people of color feel better.

FREEDOM OF POLITICALLY CORRECT SPEECH?

As I said, America is experiencing a war within her borders on several fronts. One of the cornerstones upon which our freedom rests is the freedom of speech. But, in the land of the freaks and the home of the slaves, this right is under attack by the left.

Case in point. The controversy about Atlanta Braves ballplayer John Rocker being forced to take psychological counseling (Newspeak for "thought control") is a very serious matter. Enough has been said, but not enough done, about Ted "the Mouth" Turner's Polish jokes, his digs at Pope John Paul, and his contempt for Christianity. And we know about Alec "Braveheart" Baldwin's cute witticism about lynching Rep. Henry Hyde and his family during the impeachment proceedings.

These people can trash whoever they want. It's their right. And they can get away with it; they're certified, dyed-in-the-dung liberals. It doesn't take much in the way of guts to slander religion and conservatives if you're a liberal. And if you control much of the media, like Ted Turner, then I guess you feel big enough to take on the Pope or anyone else who doesn't fit into your one-world, one-media megalomania.

We understand that there's a double standard in this country. If you're a liberal, you don't get sent to the thought police no matter what you say or how conservophobic you may be. Has anyone suggested that Ted Turner have his thinking adjusted or lose his FCC license? Have they threatened to fire dear Alec or cancel his Screen Actors Guild membership if he refuses to have his homicidal fantasies corrected?

But enter John Rocker, who didn't like to share bus rides with "freaks" and thought Asian women were lousy drivers, and suddenly there's a flurry of white coats and butterfly nets at every turn. The man must be insane. If he were a minority bashing whites, we could understand. But how can such a racist homophobe be permitted to continue in sports? To the couch with him. Give him a deep brain colonic till he begs forgiveness or ban him from baseball if not from the country altogether.

Even George W. Bush agreed with the Rocker decision. He agreed that Rocker should undergo psychological testing because of his disparaging remarks. If I didn't know better, I would wonder if the American psychologists weren't lobbying Bush and the others. Look at the business it would bring. Who in this country hasn't at one time or another made a disparaging remark about this or that group? No? Not even in your thoughts? If the Tipper Gore counselors have their way, maybe we'll all have to do time on the couch, including George W. After all, the thought is as bad as the deed.

Of course, what is really behind it all is the one-world agenda; it's Orwell revisited. And, whether they know it or not, most of our thought therapists have become part of this. It's a way of using seemingly genuine issues to establish control over our minds and our lives. To make us all obedient, politically correct automatons, with similar thoughts in a uniform world where we can be conveniently herded by unicop masters.

I've said for a long time that we have a "Republicrat" or "Demican" oligarchy in America and that most of our politicians are pawns controlled by their one-world puppet masters behind the scenes. George W. Bush is no different. Our choice between him and most of the others was essentially little choice at all. They're virtually the same, Diet-Dem or Diet-Repub.

John Rocker had an obvious problem with his mouth and, at twenty-five, he has a lot to learn. But it's not for Big Sister to teach him how to speak and think. That's what the First Amendment of our Constitution is all about. We have to have the right to be wrong. We have to have the freedom to be biased or to believe whatever we believe, regardless of how wrong or objectionable others may think it is.

Are you willing to let others decide these things for you? How do you know they are not even more wrong than you are? Remember, our Constitution was written to protect unpopular speech and writing. To protect someone who wanted to yell "Down with the King" then, and perhaps "Down with queens" now.

In time, we all tend to forget the blessings of our Constitution. That's why a review of the First Amendment is in order. Hopefully it will cast better light into present thinking than diversity trainers can ever do:

> Congress shall make no law respecting an establishment of religion, or prohibiting the free exercise thereof; or abridging the freedom of speech, or of the press; or the right of the people peaceably to assemble, and to petition the Government for a redress of grievances.

"Freedom of speech" means protection for your speech, no matter how distasteful it may be to some. This constitutional right was not written to protect nonoffensive speech. It was meant to protect what is to some offensive, even hateful, speech. We do not need a Constitution to protect "nice" talk, only so-called "hate talk."

"SHE-OCRACY":
THE RADICALS UNITED FOR LADIES' EVIL

We've all been warned about the dangers of a theocracy, where religious zealots rule. Today in America, we have a "she-ocracy" where a minority of feminist zealots rule the culture.

At the top of this hierarchy is Hillary Clinton, followed by others, such as Ruth Bader Ginsberg and Sandra Day O'Connor on the U.S. Supreme Court; Barbara Boxer, the radical abortion supporter from California; Dianne Feinstein, the radical senator from California whose husband, Richard Blum, does big business with China.

Together, they have both feminized and homosexualized much of America to the point where the nation has become passive, receptive, and masochistic.

In the new "she-ocracy," the overt target for every piece of legislation seems to be the white, heterosexual, taxpaying, working male.

Recent hate-crime legislation, of course, was a payoff to the homosexual lobby pushed through Congress by those in the she-ocracy with deep ties to the House and Senate. The next step, of course, will be to go a step further in the hate-crime legislation to further feminize the white, heterosexual male.

In addition to the laws on the books, we will no doubt see laws along the lines of those passed in South Africa, which has some of the most stringent hate crime legislation in the world.

We're well on our way down that path already. Special laws against homophobic and racially motivated crimes have already been passed in the United States. It won't be long before we, like South Africa, expand such crimes to include offensive language and then establish "equality courts" to prosecute this new crime.

In these courts, anyone can bring an action against you and, unlike America's current system of justice, you're found guilty until proven innocent. It's up to the defendant to prove he is in the right. If you can't prove your innocence in South Africa, you must pay a fine and perhaps serve jail time. The offense can be almost anything anyone dislikes about what you say.

In South Africa, as a result of the she-ocracy and the hate crimes laws, it is now a bad thing, yes, a hate crime, to say that someone is obese. It is also a crime to say such felonious things as someone is elderly, married, youthful, disabled, aged, or gay. These are the new "four-letter" words in South Africa.

You do have to give them credit for being thorough in South Africa. What you *say* is motivated by what you *think*, isn't it? So next they'll police your thoughts. Those dark, subliminal motives lurking behind what you say can now fall under official scrutiny. Not only that, but your facial expressions and body language, too.

Do you really want to live in a country where you can't speak— even think—freely, like in South Africa? After all, this is really what the self-deluded liberal heads of our new she-ocracy want for us—the Boxers, Feinsteins, and hateful Hillary. Hear me. Anyone who pushes such hate crime legislation jeopardizes one of the pillars that makes America great.

As Supreme Court Justice Oliver Wendell Holmes expressed fifty years ago, "If there is any principle of the Constitution that more imperatively calls for attachment than any other, it is the principle of free thought—not free thought for those who agree with us, but freedom for the thought that we hate."

LIBERTÉ, EQUALITÉ, BIGOTRÉ: THE NEW WHORLED ORDER

America first, or there will be no world left—that is, a world with any justice, dignity, or freedom. There will be nowhere to go and nowhere to hide. When America goes, the world goes with it; we'll go into a thousand years of darkness. It may not happen tomorrow or maybe even in our lifetime, but if this country goes, it will be the end.

Like decaying civilizations of the past, America's fall will come from the decadence within and the security threats from without. Like them, we are bombarded by decadence and false causes in the headlines every day: we hear about racial profiling, gay and lesbian rights, racism and feminism, abortion rights and animal rights and guns and the environment, as if there were no other issues in this country, or in the universe, for that matter. They have become the sunspots that blind us. It's like the insane beating of a drum that drives out all rational thought.

Racist monsters are trying to shake the pillars of this country. And from the outside there are repeated threats of atomic attacks. Can such a nation as this survive? Even Jesus observed, "Every kingdom divided against itself will be ruined, and every city or household divided against itself will not stand" (Matt. 12:25 NIV).

How much can we take of this before the nation has a nervous breakdown?

The liberal agenda includes a world government that will not tolerate U.S. laws or interference; a single world military that could enter the United States at whim and arrest you without due cause; a world court that will impose laws without the protections of the U.S. Constitution; world taxes, where our money will be seized and given to Third World countries; and a world religion that will probably be Gaia with the rainbow flag.

The liberal agenda also includes the brain beating of your children, taking away your right to own guns, taking away private property, encouraging deviant sexual behavior, favoring plants and animals over human beings, and greatly expanding the "right" to kill the unborn.

It is all about one oppressive central government ruling the whole world. This is the *utopia* the left has in mind for us. Some leftists don't understand that they are the battering ram against the moral underpinnings of America. They don't understand that they will be among the first to go when our self-appointed liberators take over. There will be no "rights groups" of any kind tolerated in a future New World Order; for, just as under Brother Stalin, Elder Adolf, and Uncle Mao, all "rights" will be decided for us. If you think you have any special "rights," you will be eliminated as an enemy of the people or at least committed to a reeducation camp.

The same goes for the "fe*man*ists," terrorist apologists, the cougar-cuddlers, the race-baiters, and the other leg-crossers on the evening news. Do you think for a moment they will be tolerated? Like the other radical rights groups, they will be trashed once they've served their purpose, which is to create hatred, disunity, and decadence, so that jackbooted Bib Mother can rescue us. Who will be able to resist once they've disarmed and emasculated us and plunged us into a cesspool of moral chaos?

I can guarantee that this is how it's going to happen. The liberationists march around thinking they are freeing themselves and functioning on their own behalf, but I hear their chains rattling.

As in decadent France, in the boy-man love capital of the New Whorled Order, we will soon see the devolution of Liberté, Equalité, Fraternité into "Liberté, Equalité, Perversité"—while we are pulled, not led, into one thousand years of darkness. Do you think I exaggerate the situation? Read on.

SEX CHANGES IN SAN FRANCISCO

The unenlightened, provincial, "progressive" lemmings leading San Francisco have taken another giant leap backward in deciding to pay for sex-change surgery and all the "counseling" and hormone shots for "Tommys" who want to be "Bettys" and for "Barbaras" who really want to be "Willys."

"This is very much a civil rights issue," said one of the city's stupidvisors. "This is about equal benefits for equal work." Equating sexual insanity with race is a dangerous and demeaning precedent. There is no historical, anthropological, or medical evidence supporting such surgical insanity. Except for religious-inspired mutilation, had the ancients encountered a man holding a knife to his penis they would have restrained him as mad and constrained him to prevent such self-violence.

In Sicko-Frisco, such insanity is now encouraged and is covered by the city's "health plan." But changing sex is not cheap. For males changing to females, surgery costs about $37,000. For deranged females who wish to become males, the price is $77,000.

Radical socialists hope to propel this travesty. "This action will help lead to the elimination of discrimination against transgender people and hopefully will be a model for employers across the United States," said one such socialist, a sort of "enforcer" for the San Francisco Human Rights Commission.

Currently only a handful of nations with socialized medicine offer this medical travesty of self-mutilation. Among them are the Netherlands, Denmark, and some Canadian provinces.

The hypocrisy and outright thievery of scarce health benefits screams out from the headlines. Here we have the same phony "liberals" who hawk the need for "prescription drugs for the elderly," health care benefits for illegal aliens and poor children now robbing these needy citizens to serve a radical and insane fringe of self-mutilators.

Under the guise of "civil rights" and "human rights," we are being robbed as a society.

Excellence is replaced by expedience.

Moral purity is equated with utter decadence.

Today, we see those wishing to have themselves surgically mutilated equated with the great leaders of the civil rights movement, such as Martin Luther King.

I don't buy it. Nor should you.

All of these atrocities are at the root of why I believe America is well on her way from being the melting pot to becoming the chamber pot. We've lost our way because we've lost our view of our glorious past. Woodrow Wilson said it best: "A nation which does not remember what it was yesterday, does not know what it is today, nor what it is trying to do. We are trying to do a futile thing if we do not know where we came from or what we have been about."

Don't get me wrong. Although headed in that direction, America is not doomed to become a chamber pot. Her best days are in front of her—that is, if we have the guts to face the truth and then apply ourselves to repairing the foundation upon which this blessed nation was formed.

4

RATS VS. EAGLES

AFTER I LEAVE THE MICROPHONE, I often take a late-night walk to clear my mind. I love looking at the twinkling lights of San Francisco's buildings. They're so beautiful. As I walk, I can't help but think about all the reasons I love America and why I fight to save it.

I love television. I love the boats. I love the bay. I love the gulls. I love the radio. I love the food. I love the religiosity. I love the Disneylands of America. I even love all the problems that we have because they're a reflection of the freedoms we have. And I cherish my freedom of speech. Yes, I love everything about this country, from the graveyards to the church spires—and it strikes me that all the terrorists can do is blow it up because they're jealous.

When I compare our civilization to those who only maim and destroy, some people say, "Michael, how dare you say that the West is superior to the East. How dare you say we're more civilized." These thieves in dirty nightshirts have created nothing in a thousand years. Just check the tags on your clothing.

Ever see a label, "Made in Iran" or "Made by the Taliban"?

Of course not. They cut throats and blow things up. And that's it. But we're supposed to "be sensitive" and "understanding" of their multiculturalism. We're supposed to view the enslavement of women

43

in Afghanistan as no less equal to the freedoms in America. The mass mutilation of a woman's genitalia is a cultural "choice."

I refuse to buy the lie. And so, as I walked this particular evening, I considered the backdrop of worldwide terrorism and saw a portrait of two Americas emerging within our shores: the Rats vs. the Eagles.

Who are the Eagles?

They're the men, women, boys, and girls who love America. They would die, if necessary, to preserve the endless freedoms this nation enjoys. These patriots stand behind the brave soldiers who, without hesitation, are taking up arms to defend America. Eagles resonate with the words spoken by former President Ronald Reagan: "Double—no triple—our troubles and we'd still be better off than any other people on earth."

The Eagles know there's never been a civilization as great, as creative, as inventive, as generous, as benevolent, nor as committed to justice as the United States of America. The Eagles soar bravely into the future because they never lose sight of the history, the values, and the people who laid the foundation for their country.

The opposing position is held by the Rats who, for decades, have feasted on a steady diet of ultraliberalism. Their viewpoint can be best summarized with the words of Sigmund Freud: "America is a mistake, a giant mistake!"

Who are these Rats?

They're the liberal wing of the media, of education, and of politics. They're the whacked-out special-interest groups, the deluded peaceniks, and the Commu-Nazi ACLU turncoats. And while traitors like the Taliban Rat Boy from un-Fairfax, California provide an interesting freak show for the sheeple, we cannot afford to overlook what the Rats and their internal terrorist movement is doing to sabotage our homeland.

Let me give you a few examples of how some Rats in the media are determined to undermine America's war on terrorism.

BIASED LIBERAL NEWS UNDERMINES AMERICA

When I was a kid, I loved to watch television, as my mother will attest. I used to come home from school and do my homework. When I was finished, I'd get the tray with the steak and French fries, you know the cardio-toxic diet that should have killed me at twelve, and then I'd watch the news. I used to love it.

I've always been a news fanatic. I didn't know it at the time, but in my day, the local station would show the weather vane before the news came on. It pictured arrows pointing north, east, west, and south. Since then, I've heard it said that the word *news* is an acronym for north, east, west, and south.

In other words, the "news" is a collection of stories from around the world. *How* a newscaster presents the stories from around the world is a very personal matter. Some do it with a little humor, some do it with a little sarcasm, some do it with a little this and a little that. In every case, a newscaster will present the information from either a liberal or conservative news-slant, or bias.

Today, as you well know, many newscasters and leg-crossers intentionally misrepresent the facts of a story in order to influence public opinion. Look at Rat Boy. He's a traitor by any definition. He had sympathy for those who blew up the USS *Cole*—that is a fact reported by his own dad. In fact, his father's on tape saying that. Anyone in the media who does not refer to Rat Boy as a traitor is a distorter of the facts and a propagandist for him.

The *Old York Times* is the prototype for liberal media bias.

As I read that newspaper, I must read with my scanner and my filters in place. I have to search between the lines to get to the truth. I've got to ask: What did they leave out? What did they feature? Who did they interview for the story? And why? How did they frame the news? Come to think of it, I should invent a liberal-bias decoder ring.

Don't get me wrong. They have a right to be biased. I'm biased.

At least I don't attempt to disguise my bias. Michael Savage comes to you with a straight, up-front warning label.

I'm an independent conservative.

Can't the *Old York Times* put a caveat on the front page that says, "Buyer Beware: Biased Liberal Viewpoint"? At least you'd know what you're getting; you'd understand why everything they print resembles a page out of Trotsky's, Lenin's, or Kerensky's playbook. Frankly, their coverage of the war on terrorism is nothing short of inexcusable.

When it comes to TV, the worst of the bunch is CNN. That's why I renamed them TNN—the Taliban News Network. And most recently, the Crescent News Network because of their worship of Arafat and hatred for Israel. Why do I ridicule them? Because they are destroying our war effort. Let me give you an example. I remember watching CNN's Nick Robertson, a reporter traveling with the Taliban. He's a British snit who looks like a towel boy in a bathhouse.

Here's what I heard while watching his CNN report. I'm going to paraphrase it for you:

Wolf Blitzer's bearded mug shot fills the screen. He says, "Let's go to Afghanistan, to Nick Robertson. It has been said that despite five weeks of heavy bombing the Taliban is still strong. How's their morale, Nick?"

We hear thirty seconds of delay.

"Yes, Wolfy, their morale is astonishingly good, despite the bombing. Let's go to one of the soldiers right now:

We kill America. We kill you. You can't hurt us, come on over.
Death to the infidels—

"Well, that's it, Wolfy. The Taliban is stronger than ever. They're powerful, and they're ready for more. Back to you at CNN headquarters."

As I sat on my sofa, I shook my head in disbelief. I thought, *I can't believe I just watched this junk. How could this be going on in my country?* Never before have the media aligned themselves with those who would rape the country as has CNN during this crisis. When I see CNN aiding and abetting the enemy, I flash back to World War II. I guarantee, the journalists during that conflict would have at least considered the impact of their story on the military effort.

Picture yourself as one of our boys during World War II. You sit frightened, huddled inside a landing craft. You're frightened of the enemy—of course, to be scared in battle is a natural human reaction. To be fearful doesn't mean you can't be a good fighter. You're going to face that fear, you're going to channel the adrenaline it produces, and you're gonna fight like hell to win.

As your boat moves deeper into enemy territory, the fear wells up inside your gut. It's a fear that you're going to get hurt or you're gonna lose. Or worse, you may never see the faces of your kids or your spouse again. Don't let anyone lie to you. If you're a young guy, you know I'm telling you the truth.

Now I ask you, as one of the Americans in that landing craft, what would you be feeling if you had seen a newsman from CNN offering this report: "I can see the Japanese are dug in here very well, Wolfy. I want to tell you they've got these fifty calibers and they've got the 82mm and they've really never looked better despite our aerial bombardment for three days, and despite those sixteen-inch guns, Wolfy. No matter what it looked like from your ship, none of these men were harmed and they never looked better, they've never been stronger. And now back to you in Atlanta, Wolfy Blitzer."

That's the level of insanity "modern" journalism has sunk to.

How does CNN get away with it? Answer: Because a madman apparently lets them get away with it. A mad lunatic who made billions of dollars in America seems to hate his own country. But, the problem isn't limited to the founding mind-set of Ted Turner.

Turn on MSNBC and you'll find the mind-slut with a big pair of glasses that they sent to Afghanistan. She looks like she went from porno into reporting. See, when they get over forty they go into news. What happens is, from twenty to thirty they do porno; from thirty to forty they do weather; and then from forty to fifty they go into television news. Afterward, from fifty to sixty, they sell grave plots.

And they all have that same stale perfume.

But I digress. Every day this blonde ditz on MSNBC* glorifies our enemies. She does it with a smile plastered across her smug face. And yet, she looks guilty. It's almost like she knows she's poisoning the air just reading the TelePrompTer.

I don't understand these people. Talk about assisted suicide.

These people are assisting in the suicide of America.

B2 BOMBERS' LOCATION GIVEN AWAY BY CNN

It's one thing to demoralize America's troops. It's quite another thing to reveal to the enemy our plan of attack. Once again, CNN routinely places our servicemen in harm's way. As our B2 bombers took off from Whiteman Air Force Base in Missouri, Wolfy Blitz's henchmen were there with the cameras. I was astonished as a leg-crosser said, in effect, "Wolfy, I see one, two, no three B2 bombers taking off. Let's see, it's exactly 9:02 in the morning. Back to you now, Wolf Blitzer on CNN."

Mr. Terrorist is watching on the international feed. He sits there taking notes. He sets up a simple equation. The plane leaves at 9:02. It takes about twelve hours to make the trip. They allow for the change in time zones and then calculate the precise arrival of our fleet.

Osama bin Laden tells his men, "All right, boys, get in the bunker

---

*MSNBC = More Snotty Nonsense By Creeps.

around ten-to-the-hour. Praise be to Allah. Praise be to Wolfy. We know when the infidels and their bombers will be arriving."

We have such a problem on our hands with the news media and these so-called journalists. Our only hope is to remember that the airwaves are public, not private property. The alphabet channels do not own the airwaves, they lease them. These networks have been granted a license to use them by the Federal Communications Commission. If we are to win the war on terrorism, George W. Bush should block the signal out of CNN until they stop reporting on the exact departure and arrival of our planes.

No other country at war would put up with what I saw on CNN in the middle of the Afghanistan effort. One reporter said, in effect, "Well, Wolfy, we're right out here in the Arabian Sea. It's said that a carrier group left today but with no planes aboard, so we assume they're gonna have attack helicopters, Wolfy, with Special Forces. No attack planes. Back to you, Wolfy, in Atlanta."

Thanks to our TV "journalists," the terrorists have good information to track our moves, thwart our plans, and offer a counterattack that can cost American lives. Again, compare this dissemination of military information to that of World War II. Nazi agents snuck around the U.S. docks and risked their lives to relay information through coded messages:

> A freighter has left West Street, going for Bremenhaven. Come in, come in, come in—come in, Berlin, come in, Berlin. Berlin, this is Hans on West Eighty-sixth Street across from the tailor shop. Berlin, come in. Freighter has left today West Street.

Back then, if they got caught giving away military secrets they were hanged or shot. Or both. Today, such people are called journalists. They make six-figure incomes while trading away our national security interests for ratings.

BABS BOXER

When it comes to America's war on terrorism, President Bush and his closest advisers have done a masterful job of keeping our plans on a direct "need to know" basis. That, of course, doesn't sit well with nutcases on the left who whine and throw tantrums because they're out of the loop.

Take U.S. Senator Dianne Feinstein. She was not permitted into the inner circle to know our war plans, precisely because a radical liberal Democrat such as she is could not be trusted not to leak that information, putting our men in further harm's way. It's really quite logical. Who says that George Bush has to provide war details to every Tom, Dick, and Harry?

What? Suddenly because Feinstein says so, George Bush has to run his plans under her nose? What does she think we're doing? Fighting a war by committee? Bush is doing the right thing to hold his cards close to the vest.

Had Mr. Bush gone along with Feinstein's request, you can be sure Barbara "Babs" Boxer would demand to be in the loop—in the interest of fairness. I guarantee it, two seconds after Babs put her hands on these national secrets, she'd be on a cell phone to someone in Brooklyn:

You know what I just heard. Let me tell you, they're going to launch in two minutes. Oh yeah, it'll be over Afghanistan . . . No, I don't want you to tell anybody, it's just between you and me, and by the way, I had my nails done this morning. Oh, I had them done in pink, and yeah, we're launching three B3 bombers in exactly twelve minutes but I tell you the truth, the jewelry I bought on QVC, it really doesn't hold up when I go on C-SPIN, you know, it looks a little cheap. It brings me back to my roots. I don't think I want it anymore. And Shuck Schumer? He says I shouldn't wear those pedal pushers anymore when I'm in one of the congressional dining rooms; you know it doesn't show me at my best. And, oh, by the way, I heard that we have five thousand, three hundred troops aboard the aircraft carrier . . . Right, I don't want you to tell anybody, it's just between you and me, Gerta.

SATURDAY EVENING POST, NOVEMBER 18, 1944

I'm a collector of things, and I never throw anything out. I'm a pack rat on top of it all. In my broadcast studio, I have a number of interesting things everywhere your eye rests. It looks like one of those old bars in North Beach, San Francisco. Wherever you look, there's a picture, a poster, a card going back thirty, forty, even fifty years.

I have a collection of front pages from the *Saturday Evening Post*. I'd like to show you what the media could do to help America's war effort, and, in fact, what the media *once did* when it was in the hands of men who knew what was what.

I'll start with the *Saturday Evening Post*, November 18, 1944.

America was embroiled in a very rough period of the war. The picture on the front page features an armament factory with two burly men lifting up what appear to be howitzer barrels—short cannons in case you missed that during American history. The men with the big arms have square jaws. They're football player types. These manly men used ropes to muscle the barrels around the factory. The headline proclaims: "The Clock Runs Out on Stalin."

The same headline, if run today in the *Old York Times*, would probably read: "War Effort Suffers from Lack of Diversity."

I also have a postwar *Saturday Evening Post* dated December 21, 1946. The war had just ended. The picture offers a slice of Main Street, U.S.A. The sky is dark, but the Christmas decorations illuminate the sidewalk. A layer of snow and slush covers the street. Little Christmas trees are lit as the people stroll with wrapped presents in their arms.

It's a wonderful picture of the America that we grew up with.

The America that we loved. Until it was soiled and made dirty by the left-wing filth who try to destroy everything we believe in. Their endgame seems to be to have America's military beaten and to come home to a nation shamed.

That's all they want. That's what the Rats dream about.

But I still have faith in our young troops.

I remember watching a ceremony of U.S. Rangers in Afghanistan. Something in me stirred. I wanted to stand at attention. As I watched, I saw the same faces that saved us from Hitler. I saw the same middle-American heroes that are sneered at by the New York liberals. I thought to myself, as tears welled up in my eyes, *Look at these straight, pure boys. I guarantee you 90 percent of them were Boy Scouts.* But then a funny thought crossed my mind.

It's strange, but they sure didn't look like America to me.

There was no diversity in that crowd of Rangers.

I can't help but tell you the way I saw it. I kept searching for the diversity that the libs have been preaching about for the last twenty years. I've been told that everything should look like Multicultural America. That's what Bill Clinton tried to do to America. But, it was strange to me that the elite troops didn't look like Bill's America. There was virtually no diversity. And I said to myself, "Where are all of the carping liberal types?" They sure weren't in that pack of middle-American heroes.

I'll tell you one other thing. And, for whatever it's worth, I hope I don't insult more than a few million people.

I looked at these average middle-American heroes standing there—these boys who just came home from the front line. I looked at their wives and children, the little babies mainly.

They weren't dressed well.

They weren't wearing the latest clothing.

I'm sure they didn't have a fancy car in their driveway.

I'm sure they didn't have a Wolf range.

I'm sure they didn't have a German dishwasher.

I'm sure they're struggling in their apartment somewhere.

It was then that I said to myself, "Each one of these boys is worth more than a thousand of the richest liberals in New York City." That's what went through my heart.

IT'S A WAR, STUPID!

Now that Islam-O-Fascists have declared war against America and spilled blood in New York, Pennsylvania, and Washington, the president of the United States has declared war on the Axis of Evil. Going beyond the original stars of that list, it is a fact: Iraq, Iran, North Korea, Syria, Sudan, and Libya are accomplices in the threat against the United States. Our intelligence agencies have identified them as sponsoring, supporting, or harboring terrorists.

The Eagles know we are battling for the future of our country and for our freedom. We are facing a battle of civilization versus one thousand years of darkness. Our very survival depends upon this. This is our Pearl Harbor.

Still, the peacenik movement has gone into high gear, having received their marching orders from Commu-Nazi Central Command.

You should know that the "peace movement" is nothing but a collaborationist movement and, like the Rats they are, they're weakening the resolve of our troops, they're undermining the public confidence in the war effort, and they should be detained for investigation of sedition.

These protesters all have one line. They're all saying that war does not bring peace. These programmed sheeple say, "While we have great sympathy for the tragedy of September 11, additional deaths will not bring peace. War does not bring peace."

Gee, maybe the passengers on the airplanes heading for the Twin Towers should have joined hands and sung, "All you need is love." Personally, I think shouting, "Let's roll!" and then tackling the scum would be more effective.

But peaceniks aren't known for their clear thinking. For example, a large group of mostly college students from Brown University turned out for an antiwar rally in downtown Providence. Listen to these fools:

> Our parents taught us not to hit when we were young, not to hit back, and that's exactly what we're doing. Violence will only beget more violence.

Excuse me? "My parents taught me not to hit back"? Oh, this is great. I can't believe this.

> There's no actual released evidence that links Osama bin Laden to this. There's innocent people that are being killed and I think there are other ways to take care of things.

Do you hear these morons?

These people present a clear and present danger to themselves. They're dangerous. Can't these dimwits see that if they were alive in 1940 and their pacifism had ruled, they would be speaking German or they'd be a lampshade?

Well, the peaceniks might as well get in the boxcars now. The fact of the matter is, war *does* bring peace. Look at World War II. The idiots don't even know their own history. Hitler was killed. That was the end of the war.

And war brought fifty years of peace, more or less.

So, ladies and gentlemen, watch out for the big lies coming out of the big liars on the left. They will bury all of us if we don't stop them before they stop us.

Don't listen to the antiwar protesters.

And don't be fooled. These Rats are nothing more than a new form of the virulence called Communism, socialism, or fascism.

In the past, they came out under the guise of antiglobalists.

They've shifted gears to antiwar. They're the same plague and pox that almost destroyed this country from within in the 1960s. They need to be constrained until the war effort is over. They can be detained for aiding and abetting the enemy under the laws governing sedition.

Yes, sedition exists. It's time we constrained them. Save America. Bomb the five capitals of terror if they don't stop their reign of murder and get this dirty war over with. And I'm *not* sorry if that sounds intolerant.

IF THE NAACP HAD EXISTED IN WWII

Again, imagine, for a minute, what would happen if we had to fight World War II in today's climate of ultratolerance. For starters, the NAACP would sue the U.S. Government for racism. No doubt they would go to Japan, the Reverend Jesse Hijackson leading the pack, to work the system from the other side.

Jesse would make sure the battalion of American soldiers had the proper representation of diversity. And, he'd call for a time-out so the girls could take a hydration break. That, of course, would give him the opportunity to give a motormouth speech with gravel in his mouth declaring America a racist nation.

As you might expect, the ACLU would oppose the war effort on the grounds that the ammunition may be toxic—it has lead in it. The nutcases at PETA would chain themselves to the gates of our military bases, protesting the fact that bombs hurt wildlife and their natural habitat.

If, in 1940, we had to fight WWII with the same federal bureaucracy and rules that exist today, you and I would be saluting with straight arms or we'd be a bar of soap.

I will stick by those words because I know I am right.

If we had the hiring and the affirmative action rules that are in place today; if we had the radical mad-dog feminists who run so many elements of the federal government today; if the Red Diaper Doper Baby psychopaths from NYU, Columbia, and Princeton Law that are in place today were around in 1940, I can tell you without a shadow of a doubt, this country would have lost World War II.

And I can prove it to you with one statement.

The Manhattan Project.

The Manhattan Project was a crash program to build the atomic bomb before our enemies built one first. Here's how they did it. They picked the best and the brightest scientists. Bar none.

They didn't look for a certain number of women.

They didn't look for a certain number of people of color.

They didn't tailor it to every ethnic group on earth.

They just went for the best scientists they could find.

The result? We beat Japan and Germany to the production and the dropping of an atomic bomb.

Now, fast-forward to today. Imagine that we had to do the same thing as our forefathers—namely, to build the atomic bomb before the enemies of America beat us to it. Just as it was then, the clock would be ticking as we raced for our lives. But there's a difference. This time, thanks to the liberals who invented the EEOC guidelines, every move would be governed by a set of regulations more invasive than the current IRS tax code.

I can see it now. We'd be making great progress on the bomb until the Fairness Police noticed a lack of diversity within the team of scientists.

The EEOC would rush to file a lawsuit to shut the whole project down. They'd whine, "There are too many white males on the Manhattan Project. Nothing doing. It's not ethnically balanced. Go search some of America's worst universities such as Harvard, Princeton, Yale, and Stanford and select a statistically balanced blend of scholarshiped students."

Tragically, while we would stop to make sure our group of scientists mirrored the diversity of a McDonald's commercial, the enemies of America would gain the upper hand and make hamburger meat out of our country.

TERROR IS CALCULATED

One reason for the widespread ignorance of the sheeple is an unfamiliarity with the inner workings of a terrorist mind. Sheeple and skeptics alike must understand that:

Terror is calculated.

Terror is reasoned.

Terror is a duty.

Let me explain why. In my edition of *A Tale of Two Cities* by Charles Dickens, there's an afterword by a Steven Koch. He points back in history to a period of terrorist activity in France. He observed, "The ideology that justified the Paris terror is the phenomenon dear to the revolutionary mind known as 'collective guilt.' In the light of which individual offenses are incidental, unimportant, or even unreal in a truly radical moral scheme. The only meaningful crime is the crime of the social system against those it oppresses and abuses."

Are you starting to see the picture now? Do you understand why the radical left in America sees you as guilty even though you have nothing to do with what they see to be the oppression?

You are simply part of the collective guilt.

You are part of the social system that they say oppresses and abuses Turd World nations. That's why the left constantly refers to oppression and abuse. They believe the system is guilty. Radical change means changing the system. Not through the peaceful actions of individuals but through collective violence.

What individuals do or don't do is trivial. Real innocence and real guilt are determined by their place in the system. Now, let's pause right there. Osama bin Laden said that everyone in the World Trade Center was a soldier. See? He's the same as the French revolutionaries. He's the exact same animal as Yasser Arafat, who orders his homicidal maniacs to plant nail bombs—the nails being dipped in rat poison—near unarmed Jewish civilians in Israel.

No matter what OBL may do, he believes revolutionaries are innocent. Conversely, no matter what a peace-loving person may have done, as a nonrevolutionary he is guilty. There is only one way for a citizen to become "innocent" and that is to become a terrorist revolutionary. On the other hand, a revolutionary can commit only one crime, and that is to betray the revolution.

Let me break it down for you. Take Rat Boy. This American teen turned Taliban gangster is a disturbed human being. It certainly doesn't release him from the crimes he has committed. Rat Boy is a demented type of snot-nosed American who seeks purity from the bourgeois values that he hates.

He hates America, so he throws away the clothing of America.

He hates the mores of America.

He hates the entertainment industry.

He hates the values of America.

Indeed, America isn't religious enough for him. Catholicism isn't pure enough for him, so Rat Boy does a 180. He puts on the garb of the terrorists and then takes on the religion of the terrorists. His final step is to *become* one of the terrorists. Why? This may surprise you: the search for purity.

Purity drives the terrorist revolution. For the Westerners, maybe it's a result of spending too much time in liberal schools and liberal churches. One way or the other, they've come to believe they're more "pure" than you and I. Yes, they use terror. Yes, they're totally crazy. But they think that they're more pure than you and I. That's the most disgusting part for me.

They're blind to their own thirst for violence and power.

They're blind to the evil that they inflict on others.

Look what they did to the women of Afghanistan. Look what

they did to other religions in Afghanistan, as when they blew up Buddhist statues that had been there for fifteen hundred years because it wasn't their "pure" religion. They loathe everything that has evolved after the twelfth century.

Revolutionists, like OBL, are enchanted with the idea of purity. Their movement is driven by what they see as a purifying rage. That's why revolutionaries like terror.

That's also why America must use everything in her power to ferret out and squash those who engage in terrorism. Sorry, you peaceniks. Lighting a candle and singing "Give Peace a Chance" isn't gonna convert this bunch to the wonders of modern civilization.

HOW THE COHEN-ALBRIGHT CONNECTION GOT US HERE

I'm going to call it the way I see it. The most maddening aspect of these terrorist attacks against America is the way the Clinton administration dropped the ball early in the game. You don't believe me? I ask you . . .

Did more harebrained *Mr. Rogers' Neighborhood* thinking in the Clinton regime blow a hole in the USS *Cole*?

Did Secretary of Hate Mad Halfbright's desire for diplomacy take precedence over security?

Was the national security adviser, the lawyer Sandy Berger, more interested in "deals" than in security?

After the hole in the *Cole,* here's what we heard: "In terms of the policy of engagement with Yemen or any other country in the Middle East, I think it's very important to realize that these decisions are not made by just the Defense Department. They are government-wide policies," said Pentagon spokesmouth Ken Bacon.

Admiral Vern Clark, the chief of naval operations, said refueling in treacherous Yemen was "at the heart of the motivation of the unified commander as they are improving our relations in that part of the world." We now know that "improved relations" in the new diverse navy means letting a U.S. warship be bombed without retaliating.

If I had been the lead investigator on the board of inquiry of that terrorist incident, I would have asked:

1. Why was the bombed ship not refueled at sea by an oiler? (Every aircraft carrier battle group has its own supply and fuel ships.)

2. Why was the bomb-laden rubber boat permitted to approach the *Cole*? Seldom are any boats or ships permitted to approach a U.S. vessel on the open seas or in port without first being cleared and often boarded and inspected.

3. Why was deck security lax or nonexistent? Did Madame Halfbright order a "nonthreatening" deck presence to placate Yemeni sensibilities? Was the crew afraid to act, fearing accusations of "racial profiling" against Arabs?

4. Why did Admiral Clark go on worldwide television after this terrorist act and declare, "This type of attack is impossible to defend against"? Does this not invite terrorists to attack our warships? If Clark wasn't able to defend our sailors and ships, Clinton should have appointed someone who could! (*Hint:* Man the guns. Establish a defensive perimeter. Insist on U.S. naval personnel—armed to the teeth—on all foreign supply and support watercraft. Too much military presence, Madame Albright? Secretary Cohen? Admiral Clark?)

When Russia fell to the Bolsheviks, it was because of the corrupt and incompetent leadership of the Tsar and his cronies. We have all known the Clinton and Gore teams to be corrupt.

With the bombing of the *Cole*, the loss or theft of the "crown jewels" of our nuclear secrets at Los Alamos, the plundering of our strategic oil reserves, we now see where their incompetence has brought us.

As it's been said, those who fail to learn from history are doomed to repeat its mistakes. Case in point.

OSAMA'S TRIAL

If Osama was one day delivered to us alive, and if the radical leftist Rats who hate America have their way, OBL will not stand trial before a military tribunal. Instead, his "case" would probably be presented to Judge Ginsburg, formerly of the ACLU. Would you care to predict the media circus surrounding this trial? Forget O.J.; OBL's ratings would be through the roof.

No question. Harvard professors would act as quickly as possible to defend Osama bin Laden just for the media fame. The same psychotics who have given us such hell in the education system would slit the throat of Lady Justice to defend this madman.

But can you imagine what these lawyers would do? It would be one of the greatest platforms for the dissemination of a hideous, murderous, antilife ideology. The trial would turn into a complete mockery. It would be worse than that conducted at the Hague by those foolish Scottish judges who could find only one Libyan responsible for PanAm Flight 103.

And, of course, Osama would skirt the death penalty. He'd probably be released for good behavior, sentenced to do one hundred hours of community service lecturing Americans on the wonders of Islam at Harvard's Kennedy School of Government (that ghetto of radicalism where Hollywood Idiots are often guest lecturers).

FROM THIRD REICH TO THIRD WAY
TO THIRD RAIL

Gerhard Schröder. Tony Blair. Bill Clinton. And now, Tom Daschle. What do these men have in common? They are relatively "good-looking," they wear "good suits," they all smile too much, and they are all New World Order socialists.

But socialism is dead, you say. And you are right. Dead as a *word* but very much alive as *policy*.

The emphasis on "free prescription drugs" during the presidential campaign is but one example of socialized medicine (orchestrated during the "debates" by that baggy-eyed Bolshevik Jim Lehrer of PBS—People's Bolshevik Service). The increase in spending on "education"—without emphasizing creativity or performance—is another socialist sacred cow.

Health and education are always pushed as the great triumphs of socialism. In Stalinist Cuba, people are said to be tired of hearing that.

"We have been saying that for forty-two years . . . What else is there? The revolution had great ideas in the beginning. Fidel was a brilliant organizer. But he stayed in the past," said a Cuban construction worker in a recent newspaper interview.

Health and education. Free prescription drugs. More educrats. Less learning. "Medicare. Medicaid. Education." And, of course, now "the environment." The mantras of the Third Way: health, education, the environment.

In England, the Third Way Führer Blair floods the small island with Asians and Africans to teach white boys about "international diversity." Instead, race riots exploded in three northern towns in 2001. In response, government power will grow to restore order . . . to protect immigrants . . . to give the English dictator absolute control.

In Germany, the former leftist street thug Schröder, a lifetime anti-American Communist who now wears designer suits and smiles a lot, recently rebuilt Hitler's seat of government. He now openly touts German power and ambitions and dreams of a European army, under his command. He is thought to be the architect of NATO's bombing of Yugoslavia to fulfill a German dream of a Baltic Sea port.

In the name of pragmatism, these "Third Way" managers push experiments on embryos. To select traits, you see. When challenged by ethicists who see the stalking horse of the extensive eugenics program and other Nazi medical experiments meant to create an unblemished master Aryan race, the smiling, suited thugs say, "Our moral responsibility is also to take care of our jobs and well-being."

Always the managers, these Third Way would-be dictators are leading the world to the Third Rail. Absolute power wielded by a few thousand new mandarins while the rest of humanity bathes in the pollution of entertainment (i.e., violence and pornography), sports and shopping.

HOMELAND DEFENSE FUND

Now on to the domestic home front and the homeland defense in this Rats vs. Eagles conflict. Let's start with our ten nuclear weapons research laboratories. Are they vulnerable to terrorist attacks? Yes. They have failed about half of recent security drills. That's right. While you had your hat on backward, and while Ms. Clinton told you that multiculturalism and diversity would save America, our nuclear weapons labs were compromised.

We ran some drills in October 2000 at the Los Alamos national laboratory in New Mexico. Mock terrorists gained control of sensitive nuclear material, which, if detonated, would have endangered significant parts of several states including New Mexico and Colorado. Whether you are liberal or conservative, gay or straight, black or white, you would have died.

In an earlier test at the same lab, an army special forces team used a household garden cart to haul away enough weapons-grade uranium to build several nuclear weapons.

Feeling secure?

And, in another test of the Rocky Flat site near Denver, Navy SEALs cut a hole in a chain-link fence as they escaped with enough plutonium for several nuclear bombs. Thank you, former Energy Department Secretary Bill Richardson, who gave us the disappearing hard drives and, of course, the porous fences at our nuclear weapons research and production facilities.

If you think I exaggerate, guess again. These details were reported by the *Chicago Tribune*, hardly known for its right-wing bias.

The report was based on information provided by twelve whistle-blowers, according to the reporter. "These repeated security breaches are cause for serious concern, because Energy Department employees"—listen to this—"were warned before each security exercise that an exercise would come. But they still failed to stop would-be terrorists in more than 50 percent of the drills."

So, ladies and gentlemen, put your hat on backward. Just because America's ten nuclear weapons research and production facilities are vulnerable, that shouldn't make you stay away from the theater, should it?

BE "SENSITIVE" WHEN COUNTERING TERRORISM

The good news—if you can call it that—is that it takes at least a truckload of chemicals to damage a city's water supply. If you see suspicious people in a truck peering at a reservoir, and if you live in the San Francisco Bay Area, call Barbara Boxer. I'm sure she'll help you.

But, of course, let's say you see three swarthy men of Middle Eastern descent somewhere out in the Heartland. You watch with interest as they're unloading something into a reservoir. Make certain you're not motivated by racial profiling before you call the FBI.

You might get arrested for a hate crime.

The important thing is to make sure you don't commit any crimes or hurt anyone's feelings as you attempt to prevent a terrorist action. You see, preserving the self-worth of all people, even terrorists, is far more important than our national security.

It doesn't matter if we all die.

Here's the most important thing to remember: It doesn't matter if you lose your life as long as you don't lose your political sensitivity and political correctness. You see, it's paramount that you maintain your integrity as a diversity-loving sheeple. Just think how hard Clinton worked to create this environment of multiculturalism.

You don't want Clinton's legacy to go up in smoke, do you?

YOU ARE GOING TO HEAR WORD GAMES

Do you think that I no longer sound enough like the good loyal sheeple? What do you want from me? Would you prefer that I roll over and spout the company line: "Well, I believe the men in the government are doing the best they can, and I think we have to back them to the hilt. And I think that anybody who asks questions of the government at this time is being disloyal and ought to be investigated. I think people who ask questions are far more dangerous than the terrorists."

See, in this Rats vs. Eagles battle, you're gonna hear word games. I hear the games every day, and I'm getting sick of them. When I see another smiling, sweaty senator or congressman in the media getting up and telling me not to worry, that the American people are the best people in the world, and the American people are the strongest people in the world, and by golly the American people are going to win this thing—I want to puke.

It's gonna take a lot more than rhetoric.

Another word game you're going to hear is that Islam is a religion of peace and that terrorism is a perversion of Islam. Why, then, are Muslim countries embroiled in the great majority of the wars being fought on planet Earth? That's an absolute fact. Check it out for yourself. Take Indonesia, the Philippines, Chechnya, or India. It's radical Muslims trying to kill non-Muslims or convert them.

A related aspect of this word game is to admit that, yes, maybe Osama bin Laden is the idol of the Islamic masses. And maybe he is most popular in the mosques and religious schools in the Middle East. But, you better believe Islam is peaceful because we are being told it is. If you disagree, you're a racist.

Here's another word game coming from the left wing. They assert the only way to deal with terrorism is to address the root causes. Let me decode what they're really saying.

You are the root cause.

Your lifestyle caused the 9/11 attack.

You impoverish the Arabs by buying their oil.

And you humiliate the other Middle Easterners with foreign aid.

See? The fact that America is a success as a civilization makes them seem primitive and fanatical failures. For this reason, the Red Diaper Doper Babies reason you shouldn't have a civilization. But, it's not personal. You gotta remember that. We just need to reach out to those less fortunate thugs in dirty nightshirts.

LET US SHOW WE HAVE THE WILL

I spoke with former Israeli Prime Minister Benjamin Netanyahu about terrorism. He artfully traced modern terrorism from the "hateful ideology" of Nazism to what we're seeing today on the world scene, with its implications for America. One clear difference surfaced. The Germans under Hitler were not willing to blow themselves up with munitions.

Today's evildoers, he observed, have summer camps for children where suicide bombing is fostered. They even have films to show the kids the technique. That reality—that level of depravity—is almost impossible for the American mind to grasp. Which explains why so many yawn when our borders are compromised, when students from other countries stay beyond the limits of their visas, and when some politician suggests we grant citizen status to all illegal aliens.

Oh sure, we knew that in World War II the Japanese kamikazes were willing to die for their cause. We also knew that they did not stop until two atomic bombs were dropped on their homeland.

But the peaceniks forget that page in history.

I am convinced the same principle applies today. Why? Because Osama bin Laden approaches terrorism exactly the same way as the kamikazes of yesteryear.

Netanyahu agrees with me. He said, "We have to eradicate terrorism the way that the great civilized powers eradicated piracy in the nineteenth century and Nazism in the twentieth century."

Which, I might add for the benefit of the Rats, has nothing to do with embracing and "understanding the plight" of OBL and his death squad.

You may think I've gone over the edge with this next statement. I don't care. It's the truth. I want a real war declared on terrorism. That means Americans must give up some civil liberties in order to catch those who would kill us and then we get our civil liberties back.

I'm not gonna mince words with you. I want racial profiling, and I want it now. And I want to know what you in the Muslim community are doing proactively to help the FBI catch the people who want to kill all of us. I have not gotten that answer. I'm tired of hearing that 99.9 percent of the Muslims are wonderful and they love America. Well, that's great.

I'm worried about the 0.1 percent who don't.

And, I'd like to know why the 99.9 percent of the community aren't helping us or, if they are helping us, why they don't tell us they are helping. And how. I want that released. I want a little honesty in the picture. And I'm not getting it. I'm getting double-talk, I'm getting public relations, and you're getting it, too.

Worse, I'm getting the psychobabble from professors who try to convince me that the jihad was our fault. We're experiencing the anger of the Third World, I'm told. They're angry as they watch the capitalists on television destroying the Third World.

What Third World are you talking about?

The filth? The dirt? The poverty? The disease? The sexism? Let it all be gone. What are you trying to protect there in the sacred Third World? Most of those who live there hate it. They don't want to be there. I've been in the Third World long enough to know. They hate that world. It's a world of disease and poverty and ignorance and oppression. They'd give anything to live half as well as the poorest American lives.

But most of you sheeple don't know that. Because you're the product of television and you're the product of a liberal education from professors who've never talked to people in these places. I have. And it was a real lesson.

THE ENEMY HAS NO CREATIVITY

In an odd sort of way, our war on terrorism has made me cherish what I have. I find that I want to enjoy everything in my life more than ever. Why, you ask? I realize these vermin, these subhumans, these animals, these snakes, these cockroaches, these beetles want to take away and destroy everything in my civilization.

And they want to destroy it out of sheer jealousy because they have created nothing in about eight hundred years. They can't create, these people. They have no capacity to create anything. To them, cutting the throat of a woman on an airplane is a creation. To them, smashing a plane into a building that they could never hope to build is a creation.

That shows you how demented they are.

That's why everything in my civilization—from the high-rises to the marble sculptures, from the century-old churches to the brand-new libraries—remind me that we as a people have much to preserve and to cherish. Not to mention the sacredness of life itself, our families, and our children. We're all so fragile, particularly in an open and free society.

Do you understand what I'm saying to you? I hope you do because our future as a nation depends on a reawakening to the American identity that made us the greatest nation on planet Earth. What is this identity? Borders, language, and culture, as I will explain later.

In a way, I'm imploring you to go out into your garden and smell a flower. Allow the delicate fragrance to clear away the cobwebs of liberalism and the convoluted worldview of the Rats. And then, when you return to your house, look your child in the eyes. If you've been yelling at your kid, stop yelling tonight, for once. If she's young or if she's old, look into your child's eyes. See the humanity inside of her irises.

You'll understand what you're fighting for.

You'll understand what the Rats want to kill.

The Rats want to annihilate everything that's good in the world and replace it with everything that's evil. Which do you want? One thousand years of darkness? Or, one thousand years of light?

5

CHRISTOPHOBIA:

In Praise of Christianity

~

THE FOUNDING FATHERS guaranteed us "freedom *of* religion" not "freedom *from* religion." Did you get that? The boll weevils on the left claim the Constitution has erected a "wall of separation between church and state." They say Americans cannot pray in public; Americans must not display religious symbols on certain holidays in public; nor can Americans sing Christmas carols in public.

But they're wrong.

The alleged "wall of separation" doesn't exist. It cannot be found in any of the constitutional documents. Period. This purposeful deception, fostered by the extremists in the ACLU, is perhaps the paramount achievement of the radical left in this God-fearing nation.

America was founded on Judeo-Christian principles. Prayer and attending religious services have both been a part of our cultural experience as far back as the arrival of the *Mayflower*. Like it or not, religious expression is part of the American identity.

But you weren't taught that in school. Why? The leftist-controlled education czarinas do not want you to know your own history.

Go back to the drafting of the U.S. Constitution. It was the summer of 1787, and the representatives who broke free from the tyranny of the British Empire were gathered in Philadelphia to hammer out this great document. After weeks of almost no progress, many were ready to walk away from the convention.

Benjamin Franklin, who was eighty-one years old, stood and challenged the leaders with these words:

> I have lived, sir, a long time, and the longer I live, the more convincing proofs I see of this truth: that God governs in the affairs of men. And if a sparrow cannot fall to the ground without his notice [which, I should point out, is a direct reference to the words of Jesus in Matthew 10] is it probable that an empire can rise without his aid? We have been assured, sir, in the Sacred Writings, that "except the Lord build the House, they labor in vain that build it."
> I firmly believe this . . . I therefore beg leave to move that henceforth prayers imploring the assistance of heaven, and its blessing on our deliberations, be held in this assembly every morning.

What's this? The Founding Fathers were challenged to pray every day at the start of government business? How did they respond? They started to pray at their meetings, a tradition the House and the Senate still embrace today.

If you still have any doubts about America's Judeo-Christian heritage, listen to our third president, Thomas Jefferson. He said, "God who gave us life gave us liberty. And can the liberties of a nation be thought secure when we have removed their only firm basis, a conviction in the minds of the people that these liberties are of the gift of God? . . . Indeed, I tremble for my country when I reflect that God is just; that his justice cannot sleep forever."

But the radical liberal socialists, who are intolerant of competing views, are counting on Americans to remain a dumb sheeple. They hope the God-fearing people of faith will forget why the Pilgrims landed at Plymouth Rock in 1620: to build a new life, in a new land, "wherein every man through countless ages should have liberty."

PRAYER IS PROTECTED SPEECH

The hypocrisy of liberalism is legion. Remember when Senator Joey Lieberman was first introduced as Al Gore's vice presidential candidate? We were told, "He's an Orthodox Jew" and "He's the most moral man in Congress." On the campaign trail, when Lieberman reintroduced God to the political arena, the atheists, the Communists, and the liberals cheered.

When some of us pointed out that other practicing politicians were also practicing Christians and that they, too, were moral leaders, we were answered with silence from the left.

Fast-forward past the election.

Clinton was out, Bush was in.

Oral sex was out, oral prayer was in.

Prayer frightens the lefties. When the newly appointed Attorney General John Ashcroft invited members of his staff to pray in the morning—before work and on a voluntary basis—they went into high gear. You would have thought he was guilty of racism, homophobia, antienvironmentalism, antivegetarianism and anti-Americanism. All because he practiced his religion!

Were his actions unconstitutional or a return to decency? What we are witnessing is the spectacle of an inquisition being conducted by liberal groups. They tried to crucify John Ashcroft because he practices what the Bible teaches—unlike Bill Clinton, who displayed a Bible each and every Sunday, with an extra-large theatrical cross emblazoned on its cover for all the cameras to catch.

Many of the senators who attacked Ashcroft because he was a Pentecostal Christian were the same bunch who rushed to support Lieberman, an Orthodox Jewish practitioner. This is a double standard. Maybe that doesn't bother you. Maybe you think Christianity—really, all organized religions—is outdated. Maybe you think religion has pretty much lost its punch and should just be abandoned. That's the liberal's viewpoint.

Ask a liberal this question: What would you replace religion with and still give people the red lights, green lights, and yellow lights? You know what they'd say?

Science.

Many liberals say science replaces religion as a sort of guide for mankind. Here's the basic flaw with that line of thinking. Science is amoral. Which means, science is not concerned with issues of right and wrong. Take the Germans. For the first half of the twentieth century, the Germans had the most advanced society on the earth at the time. They were great scientists.

They also gave us the death camps.

Even with their scientific brilliance, their science could not provide a moral compass. Science is no replacement for religion.

Keep in mind, I have a Ph.D. in science, and I've met a lot of scientists. I'd have to say most of the scientists that I have met were amoral. Let me take it a step further. I would say that most of the scientists I've met in the biomedical sciences, if not controlled, would use human beings as guinea pigs. They don't see people as people. They see humans as experimental animals. That's what I discovered at the University of California Berkeley and other places where I have studied and worked.

I've come to believe that without religion, mankind is doomed. If you were to ask a scientist where has the sense of decency evolved from, he'd have no answer. But in America, our sense of decency, morality, and society's moral underpinnings are rooted in a Judeo-Christian heritage as expressed in the Bible. Without that foundation, we'd have a jungle.

Don't get me wrong. I'm not saying all scientists are devoid of morality. I'm saying that scientists cannot find a basis in science for morality. Albert Einstein, who was admittedly one of the great minds of our century, was also a believer. He believed in God *and* in science. I don't think they're mutually exclusive.

Einstein was Jewish by birth, but he never practiced his religion.

Later in life, he said he came to believe in God because the farther his mind took him—and believe me, that mind could really go far, with his Theory of Relativity—he discovered when you go to the outer perimeters of your own mind, you have to believe there's a God. There's no other explanation for it all.

I would say that if God was good enough for Albert Einstein, he's good enough for Michael Savage.

DAY OF PRAYER

Every time America celebrates the National Day of Prayer, the atheists go out of their minds. They don't know what to do. Listen to them whine: "We believe in the separation of church and state. You have the right to pray—but you have no right to pray in public." In the land of the free, the left wants you to hide all expressions of prayer.

You can have sex in public.

You can masturbate in public.

You can cross-dress in public.

You can rub against a sheep in public.

But you can't pray in public. Prayer is disgusting! How dare you exhibit such a blatant disregard for Karl Marx.

In effect, the liberal says, "If you want to go into a parade and dress up with whips and chains and beat each other up—fine! I've no problem with that. It's your business. It's *your choice*. But to pray in public is too offensive."

That's how far we've fallen.

When it comes to the National Day of Prayer, I would really like to understand—from the liberal viewpoint—why we shouldn't have it. I'm really trying to comprehend it. Prayer has always played a vital part in our nation's history.

Read what President Abraham Lincoln said in his Proclamation for a National Day of Fasting, Humiliation, and Prayer on April 30, 1863:

We have been the recipients of the choicest bounties of heaven. We have been preserved these many years in peace and prosperity. We have grown in numbers, wealth, and power as no other nation has ever grown. But we have forgotten God. We have forgotten the gracious hand which preserved us in peace, and multiplied and enriched and strengthened us; and we have vainly imagined, in the deceitfulness of our hearts, that all these blessings were produced by some superior wisdom and virtue of our own. Intoxicated with unbroken success, we have become too self-sufficient to feel the necessity of redeeming and preserving grace, too proud to pray to the God that made us! It behooves us then to humble ourselves before the offended Power, to confess our national sins and to pray for clemency and forgiveness.

In 1988, South Carolina Senator Strom Thurman introduced a bill that, for the first time in U.S. history, gave us a permanent National Day of Prayer. It passed both houses. The House version was introduced by Ohio Democrat Tony Hall. These measures amended a 1952 law that required the president to proclaim a day of his choosing each year. During an Oval Office ceremony, President Reagan signed the bill into law on May 5.

Everyone seemed to approve. But today it's very controversial. I don't understand why it should be controversial.

If you don't want to pray, you don't have to.

Isn't that the same logic the libs use regarding television violence? They say, "If you don't like the violence, don't watch it. If you don't want to watch what they put on TV, you don't have to turn it on. You can always change the channel. You have total control."

That's what I say about prayer. Listen, sheeple, if you don't like prayer, just stick wax in your ears. Go to your nearest CD store and buy some crack music. Just put some crack music on about raping women, killing police, and burning down houses. That way you can get through the prayer.

Here, then, is a "generic" prayer delivered by President Dwight Eisenhower in his second inaugural address: "Give us the power to discern clearly right from wrong and allow all our words and actions to be governed thereby and by the laws of this land, especially we pray that our concern shall be for all the people regardless of station, race, or calling. May cooperation be permitted and be the mutual aim of those who, under the concepts of our Constitution, hold to differing political faiths so that all may work for the good of our beloved country and thy glory, Amen."

What's wrong with that one?

This prayer doesn't say "Christ" or "Christian," so that shouldn't offend anybody. Right? How can the liberal mind find a prayer like this offensive? What happened to their message of tolerance and of accepting divergent viewpoints?

I'll tell you exactly what's going on.

Prayer isn't the real issue for the leftist Commu-Nazis. Prayer is just a skirmish. The real battle is to scrub out all acknowledgement of God as well as any trace of our Judeo-Christian heritage. How is the left doing this? They twist the law to suit their goals while generating an atmosphere of hostility toward anyone and anything religious.

Need proof? Let's look at the attack on the Catholic Church.

WHEN THEY CAME FOR THE CATHOLICS

"In Germany, they first came for the Communists and I didn't speak up because I wasn't a Communist," said Rev. Martin Niemöller. "Then they came for the Jews, and I didn't speak up because I wasn't a Jew. Then they came for the Catholics. I didn't speak up because I was a Protestant. Then they came for me and there was no one left to speak up." Reverend Niemöller spent time in one of the concentration camps.

Today they're coming for the Catholics in America. I understand there have been cases of child abuse, and that's terrible. But you don't attack the entire religion and the church and God and the Holy Ghost just because there are a few perverts who should be given the electric chair if they're guilty.

Now that the Catholics are under assault, what are you going to do? Join the fray? Don't you understand who's after them?

Don't you know where this is coming from?

The same forces of evil, the antifamily pagan forces that brought down Germany and put Hitler in power are liable to bring worse to this country if we don't stand up to them. Remember, the Nazi leaders were pagans. They loved animals and hated people. Many of them celebrated the myths in Wagner, which became a pillar of their Teutonic racial superiority doctrine.

This, to me, is the defining issue. The people who hate the Catholic Church are using the child abuse cases to vilify and discredit the church as a whole. The pious, irreligious CNN attacked viciously with its tag, "Sins of the Fathers."

I spoke with William Donahue of the Catholic League and asked him to estimate the percentage of priests who may have been involved in this awful behavior. He told me, according to the best estimates, the number is 2 to 5 percent. That figure is about the same across the board in all other religious denominations.

I'm not minimizing these inexcusable crimes. There's fundamentally nothing worse than hurting a child who trusts you. We all agree on that. However, you don't blame the entire church for the actions of boll weevils who use the edifice in order to do their crimes. Would we attack the institution of police because of a small number of corrupt cops? The left does!

While CNN is busy bashing the Catholic Church, they refuse to tell you that child abuse in the general adult population is closer to 8 percent. CNN also doesn't make it clear there are upward of forty-seven thousand God-fearing priests in this country. Instead, they're busy painting with broad strokes in order to cast suspicion on every Catholic priest.

Contrast that to the way the Crescent News Network and others in the media handled the fact that nineteen Muslims slammed airplanes into the Twin Towers. Boy, were they quick to point out that not all Muslims are like those on the militant "fringe." Why the double standard? Because the media are especially hostile to people in the Judeo-Christian traditions.

I'm not Catholic, but I have many good Catholic friends, and I know that they're very religious people. They're very good fathers, they're very good husbands, they're very good people. Some of them are war heroes. These are wonderful men and women who care about God, country, faith, and family.

I have said on my show that the strength of the Catholic Church is being seen now, not its weakness. Because, however it came about, it is airing out this problem. I believe the church will expunge itself of these perverts, these deviants. The church and its fundamental message will come back stronger as a result.

Why don't we see the media demanding that some other world religions, which will remain unnamed at the moment, throw out their preachers who preach homicide from their pulpits? Why do we not see anything about, for example, the murderous mullahs, who preach hatred and teach children to kill? Why don't we hear about that?

Because the radicals would like nothing more than to see the church steeples disappear and turn them into abortion clinics. The technique they're using is to stoke the flames of anti-Catholic bigotry in this country by pitting the Catholics against the Jews, as I'll demonstrate in a moment.

WAS THE CATHOLIC CHURCH SILENT DURING THE HOLOCAUST?

It's time to talk about Pope Pious XII and the slander inflicted upon him by the psychotics in the liberal media, who will stoop to outright propaganda to force their will on this country and then the world.

We live in extremely dangerous times because few dare stand up to the idol mammon, which in our day is the god Media, the Golden Calf of the self-anointed priesthood of the major networks. Their temples are the little boxes in our living rooms from which they preach their lies to gullible minds.

With respect to the truth of the Holocaust, I want every Jew to listen carefully to what I'm about to say, for half-truths are no truths at all. As Max I. Dimont said in *Jews, God and History*, "If the Jewish reader forgets the seven million Christians murdered by the Nazis, along with the Jews, then not only will he let five million Jews die in vain, but has betrayed also the Jewish heritage of compassion and justice."

I agree with Dimont when he observes this is not a question of the survival of the Jews only; it is a "question of the survival of man." If you're one of those knee-jerk liberals who run around screaming with a martyr complex about what the pope could have done to save the Jews, you'd better read on to see the whole picture.

According to Dimont, there were 1.4 Christians murdered for every Jew murdered in the Nazi death camps. This was because during the early years of the Nazi regime, most of those rounded up were political enemies of Hitler—Communists, socialists, liberals, republicans, and any ordinary German who opposed Hitler's violent policies. German anti-Semitism then led to the roundup of Jews.

In the end, between twelve and thirteen million Christians and Jews were exterminated in concentration camps, by firing squads, and in gas chambers. There were also approximately three thousand Christian clergymen who were killed in the camps for their refusal to knuckle under to Hitler's Big Lie. Should we ignore this?

Don't you see how dangerous it is if we view Nazism only as a Jewish problem? The Nazis didn't start with the Jews. They attacked the Christian Church and tried to eliminate Christians who wouldn't play ball with Hitler's *Neue Ordnung* before focusing on the Jews and other non-Aryans. In fact, at the end of the war the Russians found enough Zyklon-B lethal-gas crystals to kill another twenty million non-Aryans—and this was after most of Europe's Jews had been murdered.

The truth is also that Pope Pious XII was not Hitler's pope but was one of the great men of all time in that he saved upward of a reported eight hundred thousand Jews. Further evidence of the pope's work in defense of Jewish people can be found in the simple fact that after the war, the chief rabbi of Rome, Eugenio Zolli, converted to Christianity. In his memoir, originally entitled *Before the Dawn*, Zolli explained that he converted to Catholicism out of respect for the pope, who had done so much to save so many of his people.

But the very opposite was recently shown on *60 Minutes,* whose lies tens of millions of viewers take as gospel. It's time that these lies were knocked to the floor like false idols and trodden upon as they deserve. I know—it's like David taking on the giant media Goliath, but truth is truth. This is all part of the radical agenda, an attempt to debase the Catholic Church and Christianity so that religion can be subverted by rabid leftist perverts. These attacks are not just a threat against Catholics, but against Protestants, Jews, and others as well.

Remember, the early Bolsheviks said that "religion is the opiate of the masses." They replaced the church with the state, and God was replaced by Communist "heroes."

It takes a village!

Now, who are we going to believe about Pious XII—a blathering earringed script reader on *60 Minutes*, with no proof for his slanders? Or are we going to believe Golda Meir, Israel's former prime minister and a Jew who lived at the time of the Nazi horrors?

Here's what she had to say about Pious XII—called "Hitler's Pope" by the media slanderers—on the occasion of his funeral: "When fearful martyrdom came to our people in the decade of Nazi terror, the voice of the pope was raised for the victims."

Here is another voice we didn't hear on *60 Minutes*—that of Israel's second prime minister, Moishe Sharat. He met with Pious XII in the closing stages of WWII. Here is what he had to say: "I told Pope Pious XII that my first duty was to thank him and, through him, the Catholic Church on behalf of the Jewish public for all they had done in the various countries to rescue Jews. We are deeply grateful to the Catholic Church."

You decide: Who are you going to believe, the slobbering church-haters on TV or the former prime minister of Israel?

On the death of Pious XII in 1958 there was a serious move in Israel to dedicate a forest in his honor, a fact that few are aware of. How could this be possible if he were a betrayer of the Jews in WWII? How and when did the story start that he collaborated with Hitler?

Actually, there were no such stories—until a doctrinaire-socialist German author decided to play out his antireligion agenda by inciting hatred between Jews and Catholics. The radical-left author was Rolf Hochhuth, who, interestingly enough, was a member of the Hitler Youth as a child (remember, Hitler and his Nazis were socialists).

Hochhuth's play *The Deputy* appeared in 1963, five years after the pope's death, during the sixties cultural revolution in the West and was acclaimed by the left as if it were a true-life documentary of the period. He depicted the Pope as a heartless, cold cynic who was deaf to any reports about the Nazi death camps. Few have questioned this slanderous portrayal since.

These same sentiments were voiced in a more recent book, *Hitler's Pope* by John Cornwell. We now find them mouthed again as gospel truth on *60 Minutes*. They will never tell you that Pious XII has numerous scholarly defenders. And you're also not told that one of the interesting features of the attacks on Pious XII is that they have emanated from non-Jewish sources.

If we let this slander against Pious XII and the Catholics go by, we will give the anti-God perverts one of the biggest victories they've had. This is just one more move among many to destroy all religion except the religion of the state.

It's an ongoing battle—one, unfortunately, that was not won with the victory over the German Nazis or the fall of the Soviet Empire. The perverts never learn. Leftism, totalitarianism, communism, and fascism are perversions, a pathological hatred of religion and the family. It's irrational and blind. If thwarted at one time and place, it merely attempts to impose its will under a new guise elsewhere. If we ever imagine we've conquered it once and for all, it will likely conquer us instead.

Never before in the history of our nation have we had a media as compliant with liberal propaganda as we have now. In the past, journalists were the ornery outsiders looking in.

Today the lapdog liberal "reporters," TV script readers, and leg-crossing "commentators" may as well have worked for the Reich! Leni Reifenstahl and Joseph Goebbels never held the kind of power over the mass-mind of Germany held today by the alphabet moguls. And while the liberals are waging war on our soil, evidence of their perverse agenda can be seen around the world.

CHRISTOPHOBIA:
UN'S WAR ON CHRISTIANITY

An international body of "tolerance" just passed a manifesto declaring that any European nation not wishing to see its Christian heritage obliterated by immigrants is "intolerant" and suffering from "Islamophobia"!

This United Nations commission, under the guidance of that beacon of tolerance, Kofi Annan, compared Islamophobia to the other evils of our time: homophobia, anti-Semitism, racism, sexism, and whatever other "ism" the Orwellian Total World Order twerps could come up with.

To want to preserve your own cultural and religious heritage is okay for some, but not for European Christians? This doublespeak is possible only because of the ultratolerance of benign Europeans. Has the pacification of Christians reached the point where illegal immigrants, who are now flooding into host nations, will soon demand not to assimilate but that the native population convert to their religion and their beliefs?

Impossible? What would you term the UN's declaration of "Islamophobia" other than a war on Christianity? And, if the religion of Muhammad can be deemed worthy of verbal protection by those in Geneva, why not the religion of Jesus? Can you name even one Muslim nation that is tolerant of other religions?

Isn't it time for us, the liberty-loving people of the world, to demand that those of us who are being assaulted because of our religious and cultural beliefs demand the attackers be called "Christophobes"? Study the verbal abuse heaped on John Ashcroft. You will see Christophobia naked and glaring.

The practitioners of this particular inquisition may declare themselves paragons of inclusion and tolerance, but their verbal assaults speak of a blind spot for just one religion.

MOTHER'S AND FATHER'S DAY BANNED

The effects of ultraliberalism and the intolerance it breeds can be increasingly found within the churched community. Take, for example, a pseudoreligious or semireligious day school in Manhattan. I don't know if it's "religious." Let's say "liberal religious" or reformed Jewish. They banned the celebration of Mother's Day. Keep in mind that tuition runs $15,000–$20,000 a year to Grade 6. People are paying a lot to provide a religious education for their children.

And yet, the PC—the "politically conformist"—director of the school's elementary division said, "Families in our society are now diverse and so therefore we're not celebrating Mother's Day or Father's Day."

Watch what happens when this poor fellow, or any other private religious institution, attempts to appease the anti-God Commu-Nazis. As I'll demonstrate, there's no way to stand your ground on this slippery slope of compromise with the left. I got a copy of the school calendar to see which other days on their calendar may have to be thrown out next. Why? Because these holidays may be deemed "insensitive" or may "offend" other students or people groups.

And who wants to make children uncomfortable?

Start with January 1. The calendar says "New Year's Day, administrative office closed." I would say that that holiday has to be thrown out in the future because it may be offensive to other calendarists. There are people who follow other calendars, and January 1 is not on their calendar. This date could be "calendaristic."

The third Monday in January is celebrated as Martin Luther King Day. That could be offensive to fascists and must be thrown out. Even fascists have feelings.

The third Monday in February, they celebrate Presidents' Day. The director should toss that one out because this holiday may be offensive to anarchists.

April 27 celebrates Israel Independence Celebration. That's clearly offensive to Arabs and particularly Palestinians. It must go. Even though it's a Jewish religious school, there should be no connection to Israel or the Bible.

This leads us to Torah study and Passover—those religious holidays are definitely offensive to the irreligious and the atheists in the school. Although it is putatively related to a reformed Jewish synagogue, that's no reason to maintain any semblance of the Bible or of religion in a religious school. Certainly not if you're worried about offending people.

July 4 is Independence Day. That must be banned, because "guns" were used in the American Revolution. As you know, guns hurt people. Guns teach boys to be men.

Then you have the first Monday in September, Labor Day. That is definitely very insensitive to multinationals who like to exploit labor.

It goes without saying, the slew of religious holidays should be looked at very carefully because they may offend those who go to the school but who are not Jewish. Such holidays are sure to make some students "uncomfortable."

The second Monday in October is Columbus Day. There's no question that Columbus Day is "hurtful" to indigenous people.

Let's not overlook Thanksgiving. We all know that Thanksgiving is definitely offensive to Amerinds and turkeys. Thanksgiving must go. Come to think of it, while the director of the school has banned Mother's Day and Father's Day in the name of religious sensitivity, when it comes right down to it, they really can't afford to have any holidays.

HOW KWANZAA CONS YOU

In the leftist-leaning America of today, you're free to believe whatever you want about religion—unless you're Jewish or a Christian—even if it's a complete fabrication. Take the celebration of the politically correct Kwanzaa.

If you're black and believe in Kwanzaa, would you drop the celebration if you learned it's a complete invention—straight out of Orwell, not out of Africa? Would you give up the candles, incense, and the other paraphernalia that you enjoy so much if you discovered that it's a bogus holiday?

This is what the founder himself, Ron Karenga, had to say about Kwanzaa in a *Washington Post* interview of many years ago: "People think it's African, but it's not. I came up with Kwanzaa because black people wouldn't celebrate it if they knew it was American. Also, I put it around Christmas because I knew that's when a lot of Bloods were partying."

But nowadays this simple fact, admitted by Karenga himself, is ignored by the press. In fact, most of the criminal records of Karenga, a former radical black-student leader who later became a Marxist and a professor of Black Studies, have been ignored and have disappeared. Paul Mulshine, one of the few reporters to research Karenga's past, found the records had been destroyed; only a few press accounts exist to confirm Karenga's history—which suits the liberals just fine. The left media and cowardly college administrators don't want you to know about Karenga's felonious past in the radical sixties and seventies or that Kwanzaa is a bogus holiday.

They want to hide the fact that Kwanzaa has become just one more white-liberal manipulation of blacks instead of a legitimate holiday for them. It fits the leftist paranoia that blacks have been robbed of their heritage by the mean and cruel whites. It's just one more gimmick to stir up racial hatred in this country in preparation for the Orwellian paradise the Red Diaper Doper Babies have in store for us.

If we follow the lies of the liberal fanatics, then most Americans today, including whites, would have to conclude that they've been "robbed" of their roots as well. Few of us celebrate the same holidays or continue the same customs as our old-world ancestors. Maybe once a year we should join hands, dance around the phallus, and bow to the moon.

Karenga and the other "Black Roots" people didn't get their geography straight, either. Somehow they latched onto Swahili as their ancestral tongue. Just look at your map. Swahili is a language of the African east coast. Yet most of the African slaves in America were from the west coast, thousands of miles away, where they spoke completely different languages and had very different customs from the east.

I do want to say this about Kwanzaa: I admire Karenga's imagination in inventing it, but I certainly wouldn't celebrate a bogus holiday myself. Anyone who can create a religion in his own time and sell the cards, candles, and paraphernalia, and make a go of it, must be a gifted entrepreneur.

My research also tells me that Karenga is not a racist. In fact, the best research on Ron Karenga reveals no violence against whites by him or his followers. He had an excellent relationship with former Los Angeles Mayor Sam Yorty. He met with then Governor Ronald Reagan and other white politicians. But, according to the research, Karenga did have strong contempt for other blacks.

In any event, we live in a country where we have freedom of religion, so Maulana ("Master Teacher") Karenga (born Ron N. Everett) can believe and practice whatever he wants. You have the right to worship anything at all. You can even prostrate yourself before chicken feathers mixed with the blood of a cow if that's your belief.

It's your right.

Freedom of conscience is the most important fundament of this nation. It's something no one else can decide for you. We should let no one take it from us. God will be the final arbiter.

When the Bolsheviks seized power in Russia, religion was attacked first, labeled as the "opiate of the masses"! Hitler attacked the church in Germany, making himself God, and the Nazi Party the new state church.

I'm beginning to wonder if even a bogus religion may be preferable to a demonic, soulless bureaucracy run by smiling talkers of doublespeak.

MORE RELIGION, LESS SEX

Listen to this, will you please, you liberals on medical marijuana who protest all that is good, wholesome, and pure. America has entered what I'd call the Mangled Century. All you have to do is walk around an average mall to understand what a degenerate nation we've become and why I believe we are entering a troubled century. Everywhere you turn you see a reflection of Jerry Springer's syndicated freak show.

Look at the bisexual clothing stores.

Look at the cross-dressing boutiques.

Look at the multicolored-condom stores.

Look how the young mall rats rush to assume the latest Calvin Klein waif-on-drugs or Abercrombie & Fitch lesbo of the month club persona. I'm telling you, even Hugh Hefner would blush at what some of these merchants are selling kids. We have a society that has gone so backward we glorify the sickos.

If you're a junkie, you're better than the straight man.

If you molest boys, you're better than a Boy Scout.

If you're a criminal, you're better than a cop.

If you're a man of vice, you're better than a man of virtue.

If you're a pervert, you're better than the straight and narrow.

You get the picture? How did this happen? As I've said, liberalism is a mental disorder. You don't take the great men and then elevate them to where they should be. Instead, you take the low men and elevate them to where they shouldn't be.

For example if, as a person of faith, you dare speak in favor of sexual restraint, the leftists say: "Don't impose your morality on us." Meanwhile, these secular humanists are having a field day "porning" America with their oversexed vision of society.

The truth is, this obsession with sex in America shares a parallel universe in the Middle East—only to the opposite extreme.

Here's how I see it. One man's opinion. I don't mean to be insulting; I really don't.

On one side, there's too little sex. That's them.

On the other side, there's too much sex. That's us.

On one side, there's too little religion. That's us.

On the other side, there's too much religion. That's them.

It seems the answer is something in between. America needs more religion and less sex. The Middle East needs less religion and more sex. How do we rectify the situation?

I say, drop millions of copies of *Playboy* over the nations in the Middle East along with millions of tiny, airline bottles of booze, and maybe, just maybe, they'll celebrate their marriages more often and spend less time fighting.

Meanwhile, here in America, stop giving out condoms when the kids go to the institutions of lower living—you used to know them as the institutions of higher learning like Harvard, Yale, and Princeton. But today they're nothing but glorified cathouses.

Instead of passing around condoms and "safe-sex kits" at the "orientation" sessions led by the clipped-haired, mean-faced provosts, they should distribute copies of the U.S. Constitution and the Ten Commandments.

We need more religion and less sex at Yale, Harvard, and Princeton. Don't let me forget NYU and Columbia—the birthplace of so many RDDBs.

6

TRICKLE-DOWN
IMMORALITY

⁓

WHEN I WAS SEVENTEEN, I had a job as a busboy at a hotel up in the Catskill Mountains of New York. I'd work there every summer to pay for college. The hours were grueling. We'd work from five in the morning until midnight. You had to get up at five to prep the breakfast. Then you worked the early bird, then you worked the breakfast. You weren't out of the dining room until ten. You were sweaty and dirty.

Then you had to be back at 11:30 for the pigs to come in for lunch. And you had to smile at them. They'd usually rip a bill in half and say to you, "Hey kid, my name is George Mosco. Let me tell ya something. See this twenty-dollar bill? Me and my family are gonna be here for two weeks. Take this half of the bill—" I promise, this really happened. He'd say, "Give us good service, I'll give you the other half."

I mean these guys were something else.

Anyway, then you'd work the lunch rush. You'd clean up only to get ready to serve dinner. You wouldn't get out of there until nine and be back at midnight for the "snack." That's the way it worked. It was something out of Dickens. You know, I was fascinated by kitchens and how they worked—how they could serve so many different meals so quickly. I loved to see the guys carrying the trays and the guys screaming at them from the back. "Watch out, moron!" It was awesome—the running, the hustling, the bustling, and all the yelling.

I remember in the kitchen there was a guy we called Fat Al. He was the breakfast and lunch cook. A fat Italian guy, maybe four hundred pounds of blubber. Underneath the blubber was solid iron. He had a neck on him like a tree stump. He'd wear a bandanna around his neck and on top of his head, and he'd sit with a cigarette hanging out the side of his mouth as he cooked. I don't know how old he was. Could have been thirty-eight. To me, he looked ninety.

One day, old Fat Al called me over. He said, "Hey kid, come here. I'll show you how to make the tuna." As I watched, his cigarette dangled from his mouth over the bowl. I'll never forget how Fat Al didn't use a Cuisinart to mix things. You know, with the stainless-steel blades that all the fancy chefs use today. No. Fat Al mixed stuff with his big mitt. He'd be up to his armpit in the tureen, mixing the tuna and seasonings, his arm going around and around in the bowl.

At one point he says, "All right, kid, throw in the mayo." So I'm throwing in the jars of mayo. He keeps mixing it with his hairy arm in the bowl. I'm saying to myself, *Some of the hair's gotta be in the tuna!* Of course, his cigarette ashes were falling from his mouth. So I decided to take my chances and say something.

I said, "Excuse me, Al. What about the ashes getting in there?"

He said, "Never mind. It gives it flavor."

I tell you that story for a reason. Just as Fat Al's cigarette ash laced the tuna, our culture has been laced with toxic liberal thought for forty years. Little by little, the pollutants of liberalism have been mixed into the cultural diet that we've been forced to consume since the sixties.

These lies of liberalism—the sexual free-for-all, the experimental drugs, the easy divorce, the banishment of Judeo-Christian anything from schools, the flood of immigrants, and the so-called abortion rights movement—fall from the libs' lips so frequently, we've come to accept the distinctively acidic taste.

But when, like finding hair in our food, we question the presence of these left-wing contaminates, we are told: "Shut up. Suck it down. It's good for you."

Nonsense. I say we're gagging on the bitter aftertaste that the failure of liberalism has left in our mouths.

No. Liberalism, and the rampant immorality it has bred, isn't good for America. It's killing us. That's the truth. If you need evidence, look no farther than the man who personified the "darling" of the leftist generation: Bill Clinton.

During his reign as czar, Bill Clinton promised that his Democrat-led administration would be "the most ethical" in American history. That's typical lib-speak for: "Watch what I *say*—not what I *do*." How many times did we hear that line? What did we get? The exact opposite. In fact, America is still reeling from the stench of his actions.

That said, it would be shortsighted to view the legacy of his immorality as limited to his sexual deviancy. Clinton, along with the societal cross-dressing social revolutionaries who thrived under his leadership, acted immorally in many nonsexual arenas.

It's immoral to hide behind Old Glory while peddling socialism.

It's immoral to poison America's blood supply.

It's immoral to drug young boys with Ritalin and Prozac only because they suffer from masculinity.

It's immoral to abort babies—and then sell their body parts.

It's immoral to ban school testing in the name of fairness.

It's immoral to rewrite history to cater to multiculturalists.

Let me be clear. I am not suggesting that the widespread embrace of these immoral actions is due only to Bill and Hillary's influence as copresidents for the better part of a decade. As you'll discover, the roots of these crimes against the nation are buried deep in the underground of the 1960s countercultural movement, which must be seen for what it was—an almost complete socialist revolution.

Still, as any Ritalin-free student of history can attest, Bill Clinton, with the aid of his socialist-loving Democrats across the country, cultivated a cottage industry of corkscrewing traditional, Judeo-Christian values for eight long years.

I warn you, if Pillory Clinton succeeds in her expected bid for the presidency, America may not recover from the further damage she will perpetrate with her Commu-Nazi-based programs.

In the interest of furthering the education that some readers may have missed, skipping class to do the drug "ecstasy," let me recap how we got here. As I've said, a review of the facts—followed by the right prognosis—is half the cure.

THE LEGACY OF THE SIXTIES

What a mess the sixties were. A real nightmare.

We almost lost the country.

The same hippie, whacked-out-on-acid heads that tried to break America over its knee back then now have gray hair. It would be funny if it weren't so tragic—they've become "the establishment" they used to rail against. Now, even though they run the culture—the media, the government, the educational systems, the courts, and the arts—they're still self-destructive.

It's not that they've ever been dead-set against America. They just hate capitalism. So, they hate their country. They would prefer it if America became a socialist country. It doesn't matter that today many of them are wealthy and drive around town in bulletproof limousines with wine, women, and song at their disposal.

These people hate themselves.

They hate their fatherland, their motherland, or whatever you wish to call it. They care not for America's great history, her great achievements, or her great freedoms. To the contrary. They think Jim

Morrison got it right when he sang, "Break on through to the other side."

They're suicidal, and they want to pull you with them.

Don't you understand that?

Let me give you several examples:

1. Look *what the unisex movement of the late sixties and early seventies brought us.* Picture your kid. With a wave, he hops on the bus, lunch pail in hand. He's off to kindergarten. When he gets there, he sits in a circle and sings "Old McDonald had a farm." Then, with much excitement, he waits for the teacher to speak. And speak she does. She applauds homosexual perversion.

You say that couldn't happen? Well, you're wrong.

In California, teachers (starting with kindergarten) are being encouraged to teach that homosexuality, bisexuality—and even trans-sexuality—is normal behavior. As the *Washington Times* reported, the California Student Safety and Violence Prevention Act of 2000 has been used to allow teachers "to talk openly about homosexuality" and "discuss their homosexual lifestyles with students during class."

Wake up, sheeple.

And this isn't just California. Elements inside the National Education Association have been trying to make this the NEA's official position for all schools across the country.

2. Look *at the consequences of "no-fault" divorce and the fallout on the family from these failed liberal doctrines.* Since the sixties, America has witnessed a thousand percent increase in the number of households headed by unmarried persons. Why? Because the anti-establishment movement bucked against the *Leave It to Beaver* family model, pushed "open marriages" and, in turn, redefined the family. Care to guess the percentage of households where an intact traditional family unit is operating?

Answer: It's now below one in four—less than 25 percent. Not to mention that the divorce rate has doubled since 1970.

That means kids today—if they're "lucky"—have several sets of parents and several sets of grandparents. I say lucky because, according to *World* magazine, 44 percent of first births are to unmarried mothers. In the inner city, the situation is even more critical: 70 percent of African-American babies are born out of wedlock. The black community is suffering from three and four generations with no father figures.

Back to the lucky kids. Aside from the time they're in the mini-van being shuttled between "parental units," they experience very little meaningful parental involvement. About 60 percent of children come home today to an empty house. When you realize the family is the brick of society, you understand why the leftists hammer away at these bricks. They would rather see a nation of sheeple dependent on big government than a nation of strong, self-reliant families.

I'll give you a classic example of this attack on the traditional family. On February 4, 2002, the American Academy of Pediatrics released a statement—based completely on junk science, I might add—that claimed gay couples can raise children as effectively as can a traditional family. It had no genuine data to back up the claim. But it caved to special-interest groups and made a statement that is sure to pave the way for recognized gay marriages.

3. *Look at the epidemic of sexually transmitted diseases and the costs to society.* Americans must fork over nearly twenty billion dollars annually in taxes at the federal, state, and local levels just to pay for the consequences of sex outside marriage. You better reread what I just said. That, my friend, no longer makes sexual behavior a "private" matter. Not when you reach into my pocket to pick up the pieces of teen pregnancy, STDs, and government-subsidized day care.

At that rate, the government could pay each of the twenty-eight million teenagers in America five hundred dollars a year to keep their flies zipped—and save money. Instead, on February 14, 2002, Secretary of State Colin Powell trotted out a line from the liberal playbook, telling an audience of teenagers on MTV to use condoms!

While Powell was peddling this inanity, the Food and Drug Administration endorsed the "morning-after pill" as a way to eliminate early pregnancy. It also said it should be distributed to kids without parental approval.

Are you beginning to see how the left works? They attack the Judeo-Christian values and principles that have worked for hundreds of years. They attack by describing these traditions as "oppressive" and "dated." Then, when their behaviors backfire, they rush to peddle taxpayer-subsidized cures. Why should I be forced to pay for those who can't keep their pants zipped?

4. Look at where abortion has taken us. These weasels tampered with our laws by inventing the right to privacy. Did you know that alleged right cannot be found anywhere in our Constitution or the Bill of Rights? See, liberals change the laws to accommodate their solutions, whenever it fits their agenda.

Meanwhile, psychos like Peter Singer, a "bioethicist" at Princeton University, has taken the abortion-mill logic to the next step. He's leading the charge for infanticide. He said, "Very often it's not wrong to kill a child once it's left the womb. Simply killing an infant is never equivalent to killing a person."

Senator Barbara Boxer evidently agrees. On the floor of the Senate, during the debate over partial-birth abortion, she said a baby isn't a baby until you've taken that child home from the hospital. What is she saying? It's okay to kill a child up until the point you take the baby home?

Thanks to liberalism, children in America have a bull's-eye drawn on their forehead. Just as Fat Al dismissed my concern, the left has effectively silenced us from speaking out as the moral slide occurs before our eyes.

I'd rather talk about the fifties.

The joy of America in the fifties was unmatched. Do you remember the finished basements, crew-cut hair, peg pants, and dancing till you sweat—till your clothing stuck together? I loved the values of the fifties. There was a father on the couch, there was a mother in the kitchen, there were children, there were Hershey's Kisses on the table. Everything was normal.

Then, all of a sudden, the freaks popped up out of the wood-work and ruined America. That was from the drugs. They traded their kisses for bongs. See, the drugs distorted everything in the sixties. Take the potheads. Pot is the most dangerous drug in America for 20 to 25 percent of its users. The reason it's dangerous is because it's considered *not* dangerous. But in some users, it induces a psychotic reaction. It puts people in touch with their innermost feelings and fears.

The potheads on the left said, "Whatever you're feeling, you should act out." You know, "If it feels good, do it."

If you're feeling sexual, do it in the road.

If you feel like it, make it with a cow or a dog.

The pot-induced attitudes dredged up sexual perversion in people. Things that should have been suppressed by the norms of any sane society were drawn out of people by the left wing which, as I said previously, has been trying to bring it all down.

Tragically, we've never recovered from the sixties' madness.

We've got to go back to where America was still sane. Ike and Mamie . . . a cocktail or two . . . no degeneracy other than in the closet. That kind of thing. You think I'm doing this for effect, don't you? You're wrong.

I'd like to see the fifties come back.

A giant step in the right direction would be for society to reward, not vilify, the people who take a stand for decency.

SLUTS VS. VIRGINS: AMERICA 2000

I remember watching a woman reporter on PBS's *Frontline* conducting a very telling interview with several young girls. The first three to be interviewed appeared to be cute fifteen- to sixteen-year-olds. But on second glance, you could see the depraved features. They were scantily clad, sitting in bed, smoking and talking.

What I assumed to be innocent girl talk turned out to be their boasting about "He did her, while she did the other guy, who was on top of her friend, while she took his—" etc., etc. It soon became obvious that they were not hookers. They just had bizarre sex for fun, not for money. According to them, it's the "in" thing to do in their peer group.

The interviewer asked them how old they were when they lost their virginity. One said around thirteen or fourteen. The second said she was thirteen, and the third remembered that she was twelve at the time.

Instead of your heart going out to these youngsters, if you're like me, you can't help but feel revolted. There wasn't an ounce of innocence left in any of them. They had become nothing but hardened, empty sex toys—and they were proud of it.

The scene then changed to three other girls about the same age, three Christian girls who were still virgins. Unlike the three sluts above, these three were *outcasts* in their high school because they believed there should be no sex outside marriage!

The world is this topsy-turvy because of the degeneracy of the likes of Bill Clinton and his followers. They think it's normal behavior for youngsters to be passed around like a used condom to male, female, underage, overage, all-orifice "love" freaks. And they treat the three sixteen-year-olds, who are still virgins, like pariahs in their own school.

The new unpardonable sin for the sexopathic left is to have the disease of "moral hang-ups." People like the three little swingers, who spread lethal diseases and kill their unborn babies, are not the ones to be pilloried. It's the chaste and decent ones who need to be sent to counseling for their sexual guilt complexes.

In a Democrat-controlled future, you might be sent to "re-education counseling" for praising chastity. The thought police will need to fix your "abstinophilia." After all, it might be contagious and bring the country back to some degree of moral decency.

When I see things like this, I can't help but have a fantasy. I imagine that women like the three little swingers are sent to one of the Muslim fundamentalist countries, where they're taught some of the sobering Old Testament truths about their behavior. It's no wonder that countries where they have strict views on chastity see America as a source of moral corruption in the world.

Can you blame them for not wanting to send their daughters here to be turned into rebellious little sluts? Even though there is much hypocrisy in those countries—just look at their own corrupt practice of female castration and their support of suicide bombings—their view of America reflects the extent of moral decay in a country that was once the standard-bearer of decency in the world.

Who's to blame for American decadence?

Didn't I say before that it's *trickle-down immorality?*

They say a fish rots from the head. Likewise, and throughout the ages, moral perversion always seeps down from corruption at the top. That's no excuse for the followers. We're not forced to go along with it. But, on the whole, it's like a law of physics in the area of society and morality. If the head starts rotting, it spreads throughout the whole body.

If your brain becomes corrupted with perverse attitudes, your body will follow suit. You'll see it in your face and eyes and in your body language. It will undermine your physical health even if you're lucky enough not to contract a communicable disease—or die from AIDS.

A country is no different; the entire world is no different.

The converse is true as well.

In ancient Israel, the country was strong and healthy whenever it had moral, God-fearing kings. It was weak and strife-ridden whenever the kings were evil. Anyone who thinks America is an exception to this is a victim of the Big Lie.

HIPPIES OF MECCA

Remember when all the hippies used to go over to Kabul, Afghanistan? The girls, who were sort of sluts, pretended they were holier than everybody else. They smelled of patchouli oil. They were always going back and forth between America and Afghanistan. Not for anthropology—they were running drugs.

Many of the holier-than-thou girls from the sixties and seventies were really drug runners. They were mules for their slimy boyfriends. Kabul was, after all, the hippie mecca in the sixties and seventies. Back then, Kabul was a beautiful city, albeit somewhat primitive. Still, it had a modernity to it.

These chicks would go to Kabul, do drugs, sex, rock and roll. When they'd come back, they'd say they went there for the holiness. Right. In their pockets would be three grand, with heroin in a balloon. The liberal hippies probably ruined Afghanistan when you think about it. In fact, the liberals probably were one of the reasons the Taliban came to power.

I'm serious.

If you, as a religious person, saw women running around without underwear and brassieres, if you watched them get loaded in your cafés, and you saw that they were doing drugs, they were doing guys, and they were seducing your sons, what would you think?

Wouldn't you be ready to go to war?

You'd say that these were the Jezebels of the West. Do you think you'd just sit by and let them corrupt your culture?

Think about what I'm saying to you.

Remember, there were no conservative hippies.

As an Afghani, you wouldn't have wanted your son to sleep with one of those girls from Berkeley who came over there. You'd be afraid she'd give him a disease and go home. Worse, the hippies didn't even leave babies behind.

All they left was STDs and then went home to their SUVs.

PORNOGRAPHY

The cavalier attitude toward human sexuality in the sixties has implications for the widespread use of porn in America today. Keep in mind, I'm not really a moralist. I'm a pragmatist. Here's the difference.

If you want to debate the use of marijuana, I'd argue against pot but not on moral grounds. Rather, I'd approach it as a medical issue. Marijuana is not good because 20 to 25 percent of the population become physically and mentally ill from it and they don't even know it. Also, there is distinct medical damage from using marijuana that I don't have space to go into at the moment. And, as Robert Downey Jr. has testified, dope is a gateway drug. A gateway to hell.

I approach pornography the same way—as a pragmatist. And the fact of the matter is that porn destroys a lot of guys' minds. Take a sixteen-year-old guy who has been into all kinds of Internet porn. One day he finally goes out with a real girl.

She smells like a person.

She has opinions.

She has her own ideas.

She may even have bad breath.

Suddenly, it dawns on the guy she's not just a life-size sex toy. He doesn't understand why she's not matching his fantasy of a bimbo who spends every waking moment thinking of some bizarre sexual experience.

He doesn't know how to relate to her as a whole person.

He doesn't know how to demonstrate respect.

He doesn't have a clue about romance.

He might even believe the rape myth that so much of today's porn promotes, namely, that girls *want* to be exploited!

The other aspect of pornography that, as a pragmatist, I'm concerned about is the degenerative nature of the porn industry.

San Francisco is one of the porno capitals of the world. There are a lot of little sex shops around, and I've poked my head into a few of them from time to time. Remember, I'm a social commentator. I'm an observer of what goes on in my country. That means I look at a lot of things, from high to low.

I usually walk out of the lobby nauseated. I tell you, over the fifteen years that I've been looking into these places, I've seen American porn approach a level that is lower than that of pre-Hitler Germany.

The violence in the pornography has increased dramatically.

The debasement of the girl has increased dramatically.

The utter sickness within it has increased dramatically.

The German people reached a place in society where they were so debased with sadomasochistic pornography and activity, the only reaction was a strong reaction in the other direction. Hitler capitalized on the widespread decadence to usher in the Nazi era.

That's what worries me about the level of porn in our society.

The Japanese, by the way, have always had the most vile pornography in the world. You don't know that? Fifteen years ago they were doing things that were disgusting. Back then, they projected an image of being a homogeneous repressed society, right? Everyone was orderly. They'd wear little hats with ears on them, looking like they came from an amusement park. They'd build little Toyotas and come to America to buy Louie Vuitton luggage.

This docile society was not bothering anybody. The militancy was gone. No more bombs. But if you looked at their pornography, it was disgusting. Girls were being tortured. There was lots of feces involved. I don't mean to disgust you but that's the reality of it.

Okay, now let's spin the clock.

It's the year 2003, 2004, and America is copying the same sick smut. We're falling to the same level of degeneracy. It's gone beyond the total debasement of the human being. It's now about sado-masochism approaching that of a death camp. And that's why we as a nation have to be very, very careful about where we go with the whitewashing of pornography.

Remember, the degenerates on the left who want to sell Americans on the idea that homosexuality, bisexuality, transexuality, even sex with animals is normal are using porn as a way to indoctrinate the sheeple—while making their fortunes.

HOW TO PICK UP LIBERAL WOMEN

Don't get me wrong. I'm all for dating, and I know young guys always want to know how to pick up women. But with the changes in the culture, you'll need an old fox like Michael Savage to give you some tips. In fact, the young guys, although they look like they're having a better time than you did when you were young, are not. A lot of them are suffering violently. I don't want to go into the details. I happen to know it.

Here's how it works.

Go to a bookstore. That's the place where most liberal women congregate, for reasons unknown. I don't know why books are associated with liberalism, but they are. There is, however, a specific way to pick up women in these bookstores.

You start at the magazine rack. Magazine buyers are easier to pick up than the book buyers. The book buyers are usually very mean. They're, like, real serious. They're there to buy a book and get out. That's it. Don't even look at them. They're a waste of time.

But with the magazine buyers you have a chance. How do I know? Any woman who's looking at a magazine is flirting. You start by sidling up to her. Don't make eye contact, guys, in the beginning, that is. Never. When picking up a liberal woman, pretend that you don't know she's there. Just move closer and pick up a magazine on any topic near her.

It'd be useful if you could see what she's reading and then pick up one like it. That's always a bonding thing. But, I must warn you, if she's reading a lesbian magazine, I would suggest that you leave that particular area immediately. If she's *not* reading a magazine on lesbian life, then OK, you continue.

Now, as you hold your magazine, carefully look for the glint in her eye—any hint that she's looking over at you with any interest. That's your moment to strike. But in sort of a roundabout way. You gotta act like a martial artist. You don't respond directly to her interest in you. Instead, pretend that you don't even notice her.

Then, reach across her face in a gentle manner for another magazine. Simply say, "Excuse me." That's when you make eye contact. Do it as if you didn't even know she was there until that moment.

By saying "Excuse me," you put yourself in a defeatist position right away. She will infer that you're a feminist man, and you're home free. You got it made.

That's the secret. The minute you say "Excuse me," if she likes you, then you got it made. After that, the first thing you do is express a love for "people of cover," all "people of cover," even if they're mass murderers.

Let her know you love all gays even if they've raped young boys. It doesn't matter. As for alcoholics and all junkies, just say that you feel they're victims of a racist society. By now, you'll have her complete attention. Maybe suggest a latte and biscotti in the coffee shop. While you wait in line, attack our war on terror as a front for the globalist oil lobby. Then tell her immigrants are the strength of America.

That's it. You're over.

THE RITALIN RACKETEERS AND
THEIR CHEMICAL LOBOTOMIES

Another sign of the trickle-down immorality that's ruining America is the war to control our children with state-issued drugs. If you've heard Hillary Clinton's remarks on the use of Ritalin and other drugs on children, you'll find the usual nauseating demagoguery. She appears to be urging Ritalin caution; but, if you listen carefully, she's calling Ritalin a miracle drug: "A godsend for emotional and behavioral problems, for both children and their parents."

As with everything else the Clintons do, you've got to read between the lines. You've got to watch what they *do*, not just listen to what they *say*. For example, after the school shootings a few years ago, Hillary Clinton and Tipper Gore pulled together a mental health conference sponsored by the White House. We all know Tipper's had to deal with antidepressants—who wouldn't, working hand in hand with that bunch.

Anyway, Hillary was quick to give the platform to a psychiatrist from New York University. This drug peddler heads up the Child and Adolescent Psychology Department. What a surprise, then, that he had the nerve to say his early studies proved Ritalin very useful on children as young as two years old!

In this NYU RDDB's opinion, which he stated at the conference, mental disorders are biologically and genetically based. Forget about early childhood trauma. Forget about parental abuse. Forget about sexual abuse. He believes mental and behavioral problems are really a chemical disorder and can best be treated by drugs.

At the conference, Hillary agreed with him and, according to Dr. Peter R. Breggin, a real expert in the field of Ritalin abuse, Hillary had stated that "whether or not teenagers want treatment, they have to get it." In other words, involuntary treatment.

So much for the idea that Hillary is urging caution.

Talk about her outright hypocrisy.

What can be worse than poisoning our children's minds?

Let's pause for a moment. I listened to Hillary speak on Ritalin, and I heard the usual double-talk. She's so good at it. Did you know, and I'm not making this up, that the Communist Chinese have sent their cadres to study her speeches? They say she's the finest propagandist they've ever heard.

She claims she's urging caution because of the outcry against the doping-up of our kids. But if you listen to the text of her statements, she's really saying they're miracle drugs. And, if you watch her actions, you'll see that she's urged giving the National Institute for Mental Health additional funds to conduct clinical experiments on two-, three-, and four-year-olds.

I'm talking human guinea pigs.

This means if a boy shows symptoms of the "disease" called masculinity—which is frequently and conveniently mislabeled as Attention Deficit Disorder, he's immediately declared ill and put on a drug. What's horrific is the way these drugs take away all the spontaneity of a child. Dr. Breggin told me, "Even with experiments on animals, when they're given these drugs they stop playing; they stop being curious; they stop socializing; they stop trying to escape. We make good caged animals with these drugs."

This sounds a lot like the work of Commu-Nazis, which is one reason I'm making an all-out effort to make the truth known about these horrific practices.

We're talking about a chemical lobotomy.

We're talking about the chemical straitjacketing of our children. We are talking about one of the greatest threats of all. But the sheeple *can* stand up to the school nurse; you *can* stand up to the teacher; you *can* stand up to the principal; you *can* stand up to them with the facts and the right books.

We must take our children back from the authoritarian state that dopes our children because they may be misbehaving.

Why do you think the she-ocracy has such a demonic desire to dope our children? I'll tell you why. Psychiatry has become the religion of liberalism. The libs dismiss religion, dismiss God, and, instead, bow down to the "pill" as their golden calf. And the dispenser of these magical drugs, the psychiatrist, is their god.

This obsession with Ritalin reminds me of the sad state of experiments done on little children by Alfred C. Kinsey. Kinsey, as you may know, was a complete fraud. Most of his studies have been shown to be false. He was a nutcase who was using children as sex objects and then writing books about it to make it look legitimate.

Yet his work is still quoted today as if it's the gospel. The same mentality prevails among those folks who think they're going to save our children by abusing them with drugs.

Here's what gets me: The educational establishment says it's unfair to test students over *academic* performance. But, the same establishment has no hesitation to test students with *psychological* evaluations on par with mental hospitals. This should not be. The only tests schools give should be about learning the basics in the classroom.

Did you know that a messy backpack is enough of an excuse to put a kid on drugs? That's how far we've come. A teacher can actually claim that's a symptom of ADD!

But there's one other wacky definition of ADD I must mention. According to Dr. Breggin, *daydreaming* has now been added to the list. He said, "Not enough girls were being corralled into the drug net so they added 'inner tension,' by which they mean daydreaming."

Daydreaming is a sign that a child needs Ritalin?

Hear me. This is a war to control our children. Yes, it's state control through drugs, just as practiced in the old Soviet Union. Only today it's the she-ocracy leading the charge! It's time teachers got back to teaching. Go back to creative educational approaches instead of doping up the class to keep things quiet, manageable, and predictable.

If these doctors had had their way in the past, we wouldn't have any Einsteins or Edisons, would we?

They were all daydreamers.

If "Tom Sawyer" were alive today, some teacher would try to control him by declaring he's an ADD kid.

If Albert Einstein were a child in today's schools, the shy, slow Albert would be called an ADD kid and then be put on Ritalin. We would not have the Theory of Relativity.

If Thomas Edison were a kid today, I doubt we'd have the light-bulb.

Needless to say, if I, Michael Savage, had gone to an elementary school run by the Ritalin Racketeers, we wouldn't have great talk radio!

ALL BLOOD IS NOT EQUAL:
GAY RIGHTS AT THE BLOOD BANK

Here is a prime example of trickle-down stupidity that has become criminal. In the midst of the present critical blood shortage, a moronic San Francisco stupidvisor protested the Blood Centers of the Pacific's practice of turning away gay men who wanted to donate blood.

In case you didn't know, gay men have been asked not to donate blood since 1977, and for very good reasons. But since this stupid-visor doesn't understand there is a point where politics must be put aside, he continues to push the radical gay agenda even when it endangers public health.

As far as I'm concerned, this man ought to be arrested as a threat to public health. This is unbelievable. The guy is behaving like serial killer Ted Bundy on steroids. To appeal to gay voters, this fool is working to have the FDA revise its policy issued in the 1980s that asks men who have had sex with other men not to donate blood.

I know that there's a shortage of Type O blood in northern

California and a shortage of all blood types in southern California. But do you want gays donating to blood centers? I wouldn't take the blood. Recipients would have a high risk of getting AIDS and of contracting HIV or other "silent" blood-borne diseases. That's why gays have been told not to donate blood. The stupidvisor, of course, argues, "One way to solve [the blood shortage] is to encourage HIV-negative gay men who are sexually safe to donate."

Promiscuous homosexual men are not the only group banned from giving blood, despite this attempt to ignore the facts. Blood banks also refuse donations from junkies ("injection drug users" is how practitioners of Newspeak refer to this class of citizens); hookers ("pleasure salespersons"); anyone who has had sex in the past twelve months with a hooker or junkie; as well as anyone who has visited or lived in Nigeria, Cameroon, or six other African countries since 1977. Also rejected as blood donors are hemophiliacs who have received clotting factor concentrates.

And Stupidvisor X says the FDA guidelines stigmatize homosexual men!

The blood centers go to all the flophouses around the state and nation and, by and large, get the worst dregs of society to donate blood. They ask stupid questions like, "Have you used a needle lately or lain down with another man?" If you answer "Yes," you're not supposed to be a donor.

Do you think these folks will tell the truth?

Would you want to bet your life on it?

Are you willing to trust that a promiscuous blood donor will tell the truth about practicing so-called safe sex? The FDA states, "We have to categorize people by risk-behavior, and HIV is definitely one of the factors."

I say that any city supervisor who has such a cavalier attitude toward the health of the people, and who cares nothing about the potential damage that can be caused by what he's doing, ought to be put behind bars.

That's right; it's called the "unholy harvest." The rotten, mean-faced, clipped-haired abortionists, our present-day fascist jackboots, are selling baby parts and making millions of dollars in their factories of death.

Companies such as Opening Lines of Kansas City, Missouri, were making even millions more—until their operation was exposed for the atrocity that it was.

Do you want an "unprocessed" baby? It's $70.

Do you want the baby's bone marrow? $250.

Do you want the baby's eyes? $75.

A spinal column will run $850.

An intact embryonic cadaver costs $400. The Opening Lines brochure reads, "Fresh Fetal Tissue Harvested and Shipped to Your Specifications . . . Where and When You Need It!"

It's becoming a huge business. And some of this money is being funneled to the Democrat machine. We were told that the presence of women in politics would bring us compassion. Yet Senator Barbara Boxer is the loudest cheerleader for this infanticide. Anybody who supports partial-birth abortion, anybody who supports the sale of fetal body parts in the name of choice, should rot in hell for a thousand years.

We're living in a psychedelic world and a psychedelic country. It makes me feel that we're living in an emerging Nazi Germany. But even the Nazis didn't sell the body parts.

Isn't it interesting that the international community, instead of threatening to bomb or take sanctions against us for mass infanticide, is more concerned about our imprisoning convicted terrorist murderers? After all, the likes of UN Secretary General Coffee At-One said these hardened assassins are innocent political prisoners.

But what can you expect? I think they still practice infanticide (and female castration) in Annan's enlightened home country, too.

Do not be a "good German" while the boxcars roll to the baby-killing factories of death.

This is your Holocaust.

IS THERE A MRS. DR. MENGELE IN THE SENATE?

In the future, Barbara Boxer may be remembered as the Frau Doktor Mengele of the U.S. Senate. Dr. Josef Mengele, the Nazi war criminal who directed merciless human experiments, may have decided to come back, as a woman. Maybe he felt this would throw people off track with his new assault on the innocent, this time on partially born and unborn infants.

Boxer urges us, in one of her infamous speeches on abortion, not to "play doctor" with the health of women by outlawing partial-birth abortion. "Leave it to the real doctors," she exclaims, with honey dripping from her pursed lips. But she's playing doctor herself, a Josef Mengele in drag.

I will say it openly to her face: Barbara, you're playing with ethical, moral fire by promoting partial-birth infanticide and, perhaps inadvertently, the sale of fetal (i.e., baby) body parts.

Every fair-minded person knows this is infanticide, the killing of innocent babies and harvesting and selling their body parts. As from a Frankenstein movie, with Barbara as Frankenstein's bride, Barbara has become a horror and a disgrace. She's sold herself up and down the line. And she's selling her God-given soul as well.

After all, Barbara is Jewish and should know that according to Jewish law, killing is a sin and not even a fragment of a human body is to go unburied. I tell you, Barbara Boxer, you may bring shame unto the fifth generation of your family.

Don't be a Mengele, an Angel of Death. The Nazi Holocaust began with mere words, Barbara. Words can heal, words can kill. Remove yourself from the grip of the abortion industry.

Choose life!

AWAKENING TO POLITICS

I want you to listen to me very carefully.

I want you to understand that there's been a revolutio   has
gone on in this country. That revolution was stopped in   acks
with the election of George W. Bush. It was a revolution   ocial-
ism, and it was very close to succeeding.

You've got to understand that the revolutionist doe not promote his cause through debate and discussion. The re lutionist
knows that the ideas he wants to plant in your mi   are not
planted by debate and discussion but by using certain   opaganda
techniques.

For one thing, socialism and communism are neve sold under
these labels. Nobody can sell socialism or communis   by saying
"I'm a socialist" or "I'm a communist." These failed s   l systems
have to be given new labels and new names. Maybe   're called
"civil rights," or "affirmative action," or "racial prof   g."

What's more, the revolutionary package must be   ld in little
pieces. Never in one big package. The sales job on you   to be done
by people who are not suspect—never by communist   in berets
or orators standing on soapboxes, as in the old days.

Rather, revolution is sold by people who deny tha   re socialists. Yet they sell you their ideology in our schools, in   wspapers,
in our magazines. They use our radios, our theaters,   elevisions,
and every means of propaganda that has ever been ir   l.

Remember, this is never done in one big packa

Instead, they sell you one little idea today. They'll   another
little idea tomorrow. That's part of the trickle-down   ch. Before
you realize it, you're on the road to their vision of r   on. Unless
this thinking is stopped, one day you'll wake up a   merica is
far on the way to becoming a socialist nation. The   back will
be more difficult than going forward.

I am telling you that we were almost there. F   years, the

115

pirates of the left took over this country. That's what the fight was about. We knew it. We smelled it. We felt it.

We knew Clinton was a traitor.

We knew that everyone around him was involved in making money with this traitor. We know that none of them have been called on the carpet for what they have done. They're back in cushy jobs at Georgetown, Columbia, Yale, Harvard, Stanford, Berkeley, and the media—all aboard! The big train to the left keeps running.

But they're not happy. In fact, these leftists are very, very unhappy. They never expected that George W. Bush, a simple, innocent man from Texas, would become the president.

So they ridicule him. They make fun of him. They try to paint him as someone who is poisoning the water with arsenic. Joey Lieberman told us Bush had armies of Republicans going around poisoning mother earth with arsenic. Tom Daschle wants us to believe that Bush could have stopped the 9/11 attacks but didn't.

All these attacks have backfired because the American people didn't care that Bush, unlike Clinton, wasn't glib. The American people feel they can relate to a man who isn't a slick artist who never made a mistake with his tongue.

Now, these socialists are forced to shift gears. The armies of the left, with Hillary at the helm, are operating around the clock mapping out a strategy to regain power and to regain a national platform to peddle their socialist agenda. Why? Why is it so important to the left to attack the American identity? Because liberals tend to view the outer world as dangerous.

I'd say at some time in their early childhood, they probably felt unwanted, probably cruelly rejected, wounded, and hurt. The children who grew up like this from emotionally starved parents became crazy. They either became criminals or they became lawyers. If they're really driven crazy, and they're really brilliant, they project their anger onto society through their aberrant behavior, which would explain why the ACLU is constantly trying to extort America.

I have a book called *The Italian-American: Troubled Roots*, by Andrew Rolle. It's a very obscure book published by the University of Oklahoma Press. The author writes, "True sociopaths, whether they murder their brother or rape their sister, have no remorse. They wish to push the order of things out of shape." I thought that was an incredible line. Does that not describe somebody who was recently a president?

True sociopaths wish to push the order of things out of shape. Does that not describe the Red Diaper Doper Baby lawyers who do anything to push society out of shape? It has nothing to do with their pet issues of immigration or civil rights. It has to do with their desire, in their criminal minds and in their psychopathic behavior, to push the order of society out of shape, without regard to the consequences. These RDDBs are like Fat Al, in that they pepper the American culture with socialist toxins—for our good.

I'm trying to push society back into shape. I'm trying to take these people and expose them for what they are. And, in the next chapter, I'll demonstrate how they are working to further erase America's borders, language, and culture.

7

IMMIGRANTS AND EPIDEMICS:

TB, Anyone?

~

I T WAS A SATURDAY NIGHT, and I was bored. I remember driving to a changing slum neighborhood. I never really gravitated to fancy-anything to begin with. But, as time goes along, you start to go to better places. This particular evening, I decided to go to one of the worst areas I've visited in thirty years.

This district of San Francisco is where the hookers and the junkies and the people of that nature generally congregate. I didn't go there to laugh or mock anybody. Oddly enough, I went there for the food. That, and I wanted to see the changing of the neighborhood. This part of town is known as the Tenderloin area of San Francisco.

It was easy to spot the changes. In past generations, the slum had gone through the Chinese then the Vietnamese immigration waves. I discovered that the new wave of immigrants is Indians and Pakistanis. I was surprised to see one tiny hole-in-the-wall greasy little Indian restaurant after another. They were everywhere. In a way, that was good. I happen to love Indian food. At least the few times I've had *good* Indian food.

I stopped and peeked into one and found it filled with mainly young liberals and transvestites—you know, the usual crowd on a Saturday night. It was a late-night joint where you can get a plate of curry for $2.99. That kind of place. It doesn't mean the food is bad, by the way.

As I was peeking into one restaurant after another, a beautiful girl came out of one and said, "Eat in this one, it's the best food around. I know, I'm Indian." How could I go wrong with a recommendation like that? I went inside and ordered the roti. I ordered the naan, and I ordered the this and the that. I ordered several different dishes, figuring I'd sample the menu.

While I waited, I asked for a beer. The owner barked back in broken English, "We no sell beer. Go to grocery." Okay, fine. I went to the grocery and got a big bottle of beer, came back, sat down, and I really started to enjoy myself watching the people come and go. There's just something fascinating about these take-out, hole-in-the-wall spots.

So I'm slugging the beer down, no glass. I wouldn't use a glass in the place. As I waited, I watched the people in wheelchairs, the junkies, the crack addicts, and the hookers go by. I checked my watch.

Twenty minutes went by.

Twenty-five minutes went by.

Still, not a piece of naan.

Meanwhile, the transvestite next to me with his boyfriend had three servings of roti. I figured, "Okay, I'm in a junky place here, but something's wrong with this picture." I went up to the counter and said to the woman, "I've been here thirty minutes, and I didn't even get a piece of naan or roti."

You know what she says to me? She says, "Next time you come, you tell me you're hungry."

So I said, "What do you think I came in here for, the ambience? Did I come here to look at you? With the gold tooth and your husband there with the ripped undershirt? What do you think I came in here for?" Of course, she didn't understand a word that I said.

When the food finally came, I took a bite, and it was awful. I left it all on the table and walked out. You've probably had a bad experience at a restaurant, too. Maybe it was the service. Maybe it was the food. Maybe both. The point is, you can often tell the difference between a restaurant that's good and one that's awful. Why? Not all restaurants are equal.

There is a parallel to the subject of immigration.

Not all immigrants are the same. Does that sound harsh? I warn you, I suffer from Truth in Mouth Syndrome. What do you want from me? I'm the son of an immigrant who happens to be able to distinguish those who come to America to work hard and honor our heritage from those who will do us harm.

Look at the immigrants from Japan. For the most part, they make good citizens. They come and apply themselves to learning the language, they take the oath of loyalty to our country, they study hard, they get solid jobs, and they make a contribution to society. The same thing could be said of the immigrants arriving from India. I could go on down the list of other countries whose people come to our shores with an attitude of gratitude. They're thankful to be here, and they want to make a lasting contribution to the land of the free and the home of the brave.

But then you've got the immigrants who sneak, cheat, or lie their way into America. Once they've set foot on the soil, they immediately apply for welfare benefits. These leeches make no effort to learn English. In fact, they take pride in *not* learning our language. They demand health care. And they refuse to abide by the laws, preferring even to go to jail. Why? American jails provide a better life than many experience back home in the Third World countries from which they fled.

This will shock you, but it's a fact: *25 to 30 percent of all prisoners in our jails today are illegal immigrants.* You better read that again. Do you understand what that means to your paycheck? Americans are being taxed to fund the cost of housing, feeding, entertaining, and guarding one in four prisoners *who don't even belong in this country!* That's insanity.

There's a third class who come to America. These dirty thieves come here not to mooch, not for the ACLU-care benefits, not to study, not for the host of other liberal handouts.

They come to kill us.

They come to poison your daughter's lunch box.

They come to fly planes into buildings.

These snakes pretend to be one of us. They might blend in as they await their orders to stab America in the back.

I'll say it again. Not all immigrants are equal.

And I'll tell you something else: "It's our borders, stupid." If America is going to survive, we must close our borders to those who come to mooch and to those from all terror-sponsoring countries. Haven't we learned our lesson from 9/11? I say we must defend our borders from those who come to exploit our nation or we're cooked. We're finished.

But in this politically correct world, we're afraid to make these distinctions. We're afraid to hurt someone's feelings. We don't want to appear insensitive to certain people groups.

Forget about it. I'll say it again.

Not all immigrants are equal.

In the spirit of nationalism—which liberals consider the dirtiest word in the English language—we must defend our borders against the dregs of society. And, we must use "racial profiling" to ferret out those who are already here who may also be planning to do us harm.

Do you think I exaggerate the problem? Do you think my solution is too radical? Look at the insanity this system has created.

DAISY-CHAIN IMMIGRATION
DESTROYS AMERICA

Californians can welcome to our fair state a brand-new citizen. An illegal immigrant gave birth to a baby girl in the back of a Border Patrol van. The woman had slipped in from Mexico, was abandoned by her smugglers, and then apprehended by the Border Patrol. She popped one out while inside the van, and presto! The baby is a U.S. citizen by law. And that baby can sponsor her entire family!

I think that is so touching.

The child is a full U.S. citizen with full benefits, SSI, welfare, child care, Medicare, ACLU-care. It is unlimited. Do you realize that child has more benefits than you?

Let's say your great-great-great-grandfather fought slavery in the Civil War. It means absolutely nothing. That child has instant access to affirmative action. Depending on your race and ethnicity, that child has greater access to the best university than your child. That's right, born in the backseat of an INS van; but we don't want to discriminate, do we?

Since the little child is a U.S. citizen from birth, she can one day apply for citizenship for her mama. Welcome to daisy-chain immigration. Carry it on your backs, fools. California has new citizens like this virtually every day. Whether you know it or not, immigration and the problems with illegals in America is one of the biggest problems America is facing today.

Eighty-five to 90 percent of Americans want no more immigrants coming into our nation and changing the demographics of this country. This might sound harsh to you, but the takeover of the United States of America by illegal aliens is a monumental problem.

When you alter the people, you alter the country.

Does America want to be like Mexico, Central America, or China?

No nation in the history of the world has ever had its demographics changed without a war, except this one. And that's because you, the male—whether you're white or black or brown or yellow—as a legitimate citizen and taxpayer, you are a moron. Your hat is on backward. Maybe you've got sports and porn shows on in your bedroom late at night; you eat junk food, and your mind is filled with junk ideas, so you don't care.

In the past, what people had to do to take over a nation was to invade it with an army, subdue the male population by force of arms, and then flood it with citizens from their own country. But today, hey, you can swim right in. You can even walk right in to America; you can fly in or take a bus. It doesn't matter.

Private Ryan's grandson is a pothead.

Private Ryan's grandson is a loser with his hat on backward who listens to disc jockeys who pass wind on the air. That's who Private Ryan's grandson is. Private Ryan's grandson lies down with another boy and thinks it's normal because his brain has been washed by the liberal perverts.

Private Ryan's grandson is nothing. And so Private Ryan's grandson will become a slave in his own lifetime.

But if you think this flood of Third World immigration is a Demoncat problem, you better ask, Where are the Republicans on this daisy-chain takeover of America? The answer will shock you. What the Clinton/Gore team did not dare do for fear of Republican demagoguery, President Bush now celebrates: The legalization of millions, no tens of millions, of law-breaking illegal aliens!

What does this Republicrat blanket amnesty mean for America?

- rewarding criminals

- more crime, welfare, and terrorism

- epidemics such as TB

- an alien culture not likely to assimilate
- affirmative action for millions more

Not to mention the continuing immigration of family members coming here for a Rolls-Royce retirement, Social Security insurance, and other hard-earned benefits paid for by you!

Perhaps Mr. Bush is living with the fantasy that many of these lawbreakers will vote for a Republican in the next election. Such a fantasy is not supported by historical realities. More than 90 percent of all new immigrants vote for Democrats.

This is a suicidal decision—a "lose-lose" for America and for the Republican Party. Why, then, is President Bush pushing this amnesty program? Cheap labor for his donors. It's payback time, pure and simple. You see, the oligarchs are all in on the scam: slaves for the farms, factories, hotels, slaughterhouses; dishwashers, ditchdiggers, and so on.

Who, ask the liberals, would do the dirty work without these non-living-wage workers?

Answer: the lazy welfare *bums*, the so-called homeless (i.e., gutter-trash) who live off our tax dollars, that's who. Make them pick the crops and dig the ditches, or let them go hungry.

The cat is out of the proverbial bag. The New World Order bureaucrats want one big global village, which they run. We are supposed to kiss our borders, our flag, our language, our religions, and our culture good-bye. Why? To make the world safe for McDonald's, drugs, and streaming computer pornography.

Daisy-chain immigration into America is a silent war on our way of life being conducted by the socialist liberals of the world. Ask some American Indians what they think about uncontrolled immigration of non-native people.

Private Ryan's grandson is in the grandstands, cheering, as his land is being overrun by a flood of illiterate immigrants. And you thought the Great Wall of China was built as a tourist attraction?

GOVERNMENT FAILS TO SCREEN FOR DISEASE

When your grandparents, or great-grandparents, came to this country they were put through medical screening at Ellis Island, or, if they were of Asian extraction, they were screened at Angel Island on the West Coast. If any of them showed signs of disease, they were sent back to where they came from or put in quarantine until they recovered.

Quarantined? Absolutely.

Does this screening policy sound unfair to you, that some were sent back, even though they were ill, and some were put in quarantine? If this screening policy seems like unfair discrimination to you, then let me ask how many ill and diseased people you have welcomed into your home lately, where they might infect you and your family. Why?

A family is really no different from a nation, only in size.

If you won't open your home to people with contagious diseases, then you shouldn't allow them into your nation, either. And if you don't care about your fellow citizens, care at least about your own loved ones. Sooner or later, whatever diseases immigrants bring with them will end up in your home as well.

Be that as it may, health screening of immigrants was thrown out in this country by our government—or, to be exact, by the New World Order. This was even before Hillary Clinton came along. The international powers that be, our unelected global government, decided they needed slave labor for the factories, farms, hotels, and the houses of ill repute in the United States. So they just threw aside all the screening and brought millions and millions of Third World immigrants into our country to be exploited as they saw fit.

Consequently, America has been invaded by an avalanche of diseases. Some are new to America and some are diseases that had been eliminated in this country and then reintroduced by the immigrants. I've recognized this problem from the outset and warned that it was only a matter of time before it became a major health problem.

But who likes to hear the truth?

Tuberculosis is one of those diseases that had nearly been wiped out in the United States but was then reintroduced through immigrants. After generations of heroic efforts to eradicate it in our country, it was brought back into the U.S. by Indo-Chinese refugees in the 1970s after the Vietnam War. The AIDS epidemic arose about this time also, and tuberculosis became an opportunistic infection among many homosexuals.

Yet this is only the tip of the iceberg, for it didn't stop with the Indo-Chinese refugees. The problem has continued to grow out of all proportion with the flood of legals and illegals into our country since then. Many of these people are from the most disease-infested areas around the world. And we're bringing them right into our midst, thanks to the spineless government leadership.

Did you vote for this at the ballot box?

Was it ever on any ballot, at any time?

I don't think so. But, believe me, it didn't happen without planning. Let me give you a real-life example of the health problem. A boy from the Marshall Islands—an area with a high incidence of tuberculosis—was allowed into this country without proper health screening. He moved to South Dakota, where he was enrolled in school.

To the great surprise of the authorities, the inevitable happened. It was later discovered that the boy infected fifty-six others with tuberculosis, some of them his playmates. Obviously, we shouldn't blame the boy for this; he's innocent. The ones to blame are those who have created this situation and those, like the major media, who try to cover it up.

The biased media coverage doesn't tell us that some of the people the boy infected were other children. We are merely told that they were other "people." And they don't explain to us how the greed of high-flying internationalists has brought this situation about without our consent and despite its serious hazard to our health and well-being.

Dengue fever has now broken out in Texas. This mosquito-borne illness has crossed the now-porous border, with Mexicans moving freely through it as a result of NAFTA ("North American Free Traffickers Association").

TB and Dengue are only the iceberg's tip. Other immigrant-borne diseases are emerging, buried for now in a slew of government-media propaganda about America being the "Land of Immigrants."

Not all immigrants are equal.

Some are more desirable.

Some bring with them an agenda to shape America into the image of their homeland. Some bring communicable diseases.

DOG MEAT

Maybe you think my concerns are nothing but a big joke. Maybe you think I'm paranoid when I say we must not allow immigrants to come here and impose their cultural-trappings on us, rather than respect the American culture. Fine. You're entitled to be wrong. The next time you're in your backyard grilling hot dogs, don't be surprised if your Korean neighbor is actually *grilling his dog*. That's the way things are done in Korea.

You heard me correctly.

South Koreans defend their canine cuisine because they've been eating dogs for centuries. I'm sure this will give the idiots at PETA heartburn, but Koreans raise dogs specifically for dining. You wouldn't believe what dog meat they like the best: the Saint Bernard. Those big, beautiful dogs are raised to be chopped up. The idea of killing a Saint Bernard for food is, well, let's just say I wouldn't eat it myself. But that's their society.

And yet, PETA has never gone over there. Because, like all left-wing groups, PETA is phony. They only attack soft targets who can't hurt them.

When South Korea was preparing for the World Cup soccer event, I read a comment by one of the locals in that part of the world. He was a fifty-two-year-old man who hovered over a bowl of dog stew while he spoke. He said, "Sometimes we become a little obsessed with the feelings of Westerners who try to lecture us on values and regard others as barbarians. But who are they to lecture us? We have five thousand years of history, and dog-eating is part of our culture."

There's the rub.

In America, dogs are thought of as human beings. Mainly by liberals. I love my dog, but I know she's not a human. There's a shopping center near my home, and I'll never forget something that happened there one Christmas. (As the story unfolds, keep in mind this is the county that bred the "American Taliban," Rat Boy.)

I went to the mall to buy a present. The Christmas lights were on, the Bing Crosby music was piped through the place. It was very cheerful. As I shopped, I saw a crowd of people with all these cute dogs. As I looked closer, I noticed the dog owners were taking the dogs into a little hut.

I asked one of the owners, "What's going on?" She said, "Oh, it's Santa's night with dogs." I said, "You must be kidding me. Instead of children, your dog is being set on some fat guy's lap whose dressed in a suit and goes, 'Ho, ho, ho'?"

This is an example of the insanity of our society. It's crazy. It's one thing to take care of your animal and to have some affection. But when you start to anthropomorphize your dog, you're nuts.

In Confucian culture, by way of comparison, where hierarchy is valued—although human beings and dogs are close—at no point are the two considered remotely equal. And that's why fully grown dogs can play around in living rooms in our country whereas they never come inside the house in Confucian countries like Korea.

The PETA people have nothing to say about the eating of dog meat over there. How do you think they'll handle dog meat at the grocery store over here? If you want multiculturalism, all you leftists, you've got it now.

I bet they'll get more worked up over dog stew than they will over an abortion. They'll get more worked up over dog stew than they will about terminating an elderly person. You see, it shows you the whacked-out mentality and the confusion of the left. They want open borders and they want diversity. They say all immigrants are equal. Go ahead. Keep up that attitude. One day they'll wake up and find out that America has—literally—gone to the dogs.

CITIZEN VOTER ACT AIMS TO CURB FLOOD OF ILLEGAL VOTERS

Dead men voting. Students casting multiple ballots. Multiple-district registrations running rampant. Undocumented illegal aliens falsely certifying citizenship in order to register to vote. Stuffing ballot boxes with outright fraudulent ballots. Polling stations being held open past hours. Convicted felons boldly and illegally casting their votes.

The list goes on!

This is not a story about Latin America. This is the United States of America in the year 2001. From sea to shining sea our elections are riddled with fraud, corruption, and scandal. Many of us, aware of the problems and resentful of a two-party ticket, have simply avoided the polls. The latest census reports that as many as ten to fifteen million illegal aliens live in the U.S.

The Republican Party presidential candidate in the year 2000, George W. Bush, won by the skin of his teeth. The Democratic Party machine pulled out every trick it had in its armamentarium. It kicked, screamed, whined, wailed, connived, and twisted the truth. In the end, Bush prevailed. But only by a hanging chad.

If Republicrats and Demicans prevail, these illegals may be given amnesty and allowed to vote. This would allow them to equal the total population of seventeen congressional districts.

And guess who's coming to a ballot near you in 2004 or 2008? It's Hillary Clinton, and she aims to win. With her office in New York City (Bubba defended her grandiose acquisition: "Well, she has tens of thousands of volunteers and needs space for them") and her Democratic "White House" in Georgetown, Hillary has clearly set her sights on the biggest prize in the land. Why else would she need space for "tens of thousands" of volunteers?

More bad news: The current congressional redistricting effort is nothing more than political gerrymandering of racial quotas in specific districts to secure a Democratic majority in Congress. Our country is nothing more than a vast checkerboard to these Demoncats, whose only goal is victory at any cost.

What we must do is secure our perimeters. To uphold the voting laws of this country, add the following language to the voting legislation that already exists in each state of this country as follows:

PROPOSITION:
"CITIZEN VOTER ACT"

Proof of citizenship in the form of a notarized birth certificate, valid U.S. passport, or notarized citizenship papers, issued by the INS, must be presented in order to register to vote and re-presented at the poll in order to cast a vote.

I am suggesting that the law be enhanced by providing strict enforcement registration criteria, so that people not legally permitted to register to vote can no longer register to vote at will throughout our free land! And, once registered, this statute will provide for verification of identity at the polling place, at the time of actual ballot casting by the individual.

Voter fraud continues as a silent scandal.

It's a cancer. It just keeps multiplying until it kills.

The voting fraud problem has become so widespread and complicated, it seems an almost insoluble issue. Multiple legislative bodies fight over "how to make it right." With one legislator proposing Amendment "A" and another legislator proposing Amendment "B," the likelihood of sweeping reform legislation is pure fantasy; a ballot initiative might prove more effective.

There are, in the state of California alone, more than 818 legislative proposals regarding overhauling the voting system. And, to be sure, the partisan efforts of the Democratic machine virtually ensure that no significant election reform can take place.

This enforcement clause does not substantially change existing election laws. This is why we have a good chance of getting this proposition on state ballots, so we the people can cast our vote in favor of the Citizen Voter Act.

What the enforcement clause does is provide the authorities with the added rule of proof. Individuals must prove they are citizens in order to register to vote. It will no longer be acceptable to merely state that you are a citizen in order to register, as is now the practice.

We have, in this country, at least ten to fifteen million illegal aliens and the problem looks only to worsen. For instance, the AFL-CIO has reversed itself on amnesty for illegals. Formerly opposed to amnesty on the grounds that illegals took jobs away from American citizens, it has a new position.

Based on sheer greed for shrinking pension dollars, the AFL-CIO now favors amnesty for illegals residing in the United States! It seems they would like them all to become AFL-CIO members. Incredibly, our president thinks amnesty for illegals is a swell idea.

If we couple the newly minted Americans with the illegal voters, we surely will end up with Democratic control of the House, the Senate, and the White House in 2004.

And that means the Supreme Court.

Remember Clarence Thomas? If you want to know just how important Clarence Thomas is for our nation, take a look at the past ten major Supreme Court rulings, including the Florida ballot box issue. Without Justice Thomas, we would be looking at Goreleone and Joey every day. The Democratic Party would rule forever, and the United States as we know it would cease to exist.

This is going to be a difficult and tedious campaign, but we know we will win. We will make a difference in the political landscape of our glorious nation. It is time to take back our country from party hacks and return it to the genuine patriots who will protect our borders. You may wonder what we should do with those who are here illegally? I'll explain.

TIPPY THE DOG

When I was a boy, we moved from our apartment in the Bronx to live in a small row house in Queens, New York. Our dog, Tippy, was an amazing creature. He would always let people in the house, but he would never let them out. Oh, you could come in and he wouldn't bark at all. He'd smile as his tongue hung out. But if you tried to leave, he'd attack you. He went crazy. He'd leap at your throat.

We'd have to constrain him with an iron chain and then put him in the basement. We'd hear him banging around. We'd hear brooms and mops falling down the steps, knocked over as he thrashed about.

But, come to think of it, Tippy was on to something. What he did is what we should do with the immigrants in America who are illegal or who are from terrorist nations.

President Bush should declare: Middle Eastern immigrants can no longer leave America without a thorough examination by the FBI. You came in nice and easy, and we didn't say a word. But you're not getting out. That's all. You want to leave? Go to the FBI. We'll let you out in a few years.

I can imagine the line of questioning. "What are you leaving for all of a sudden? What, SSI didn't go down, did it? There's religious tolerance here. What are you leaving for, sir? Ooh, you're going back to Krapistan to visit your mother? Tell you what, we're going to investigate you until the year 2010."

Do I need to remind you that we are at war?

A GERMANE GERMAN STORY

America isn't the only country who is in need of defending her borders, language, and culture. Let me tell you about Angela Merkel, a conservative woman in Germany who has been leading a revival of the Christian Democratic party—which is the only hope the Germans have. She's the kind of politician who could one day knock the socialist Gerhard Schroeder out on his behind where he belongs.

Her message is so clear for Americans that you'll be stunned by it. Immigration has been a central plank of her campaign to become chancellor of Germany. Why? She reported that "Germany is a society of eighty million people, with more than seven million foreign-born. No other nation in Europe has as many foreigners."

Let's translate that to America. We have about the same percentage of foreign-born inhabitants in America as Germany does today. In her opinion, the emerging threat to her country is: "About 75 percent of the Turks in the world who live outside Turkey are in Germany."

Substitute the words *Mexican* and *Mexico*. It's a sensitive subject, I agree. But it's a story that's emerging in Europe, and I promise you, immigration will become an election-year issue for Americans in the future.

Listen to what she says about Germany and the Turks: "We don't say that they should not be Muslims. But we do say that we are a country with a Christian background and Turks must understand this."

Muslims are now the largest religious minority in Germany, a status the Jews had in prewar Germany. But Ms. Merkel believes the situations are not entirely comparable. She said: "The Jews were Germans. They spoke the German language. But this is often not the case with the Turks."

Merkel explains that in the 1970s, there were four million foreigners and two million of them had jobs. Today there are seven million foreigners, but the number with jobs has stagnated. Immigrants didn't move into their labor market but into their social security system, she said.

That is the problem.

Immigrants are sucking the social security system of Germany dry as a bone. Her solution? Curtail the foreigners by, for instance, speeding up deportation procedures for illegals and tightening regulations for family members to join immigrants already in Germany.

Did you hear that?

But she's not strictly anti-immigration. At the same time, she wants to lure highly qualified foreigners to the country. She said, "We want real specialists. We want to offer much better opportunities. We must be part of the war for talent in the world."

Ms. Merkel is irritated by American calls to bring Turkey swiftly into the EU. You know why? She said, "Membership confers the right to work freely within the Union. Millions more Turks could pour into Germany. Imagine taking away the border between Mexico and the United States. It is just not possible in the foreseeable future."

Ms. Merkel, why don't you run for the president of the United States of America?

I maintain that ethnic diversity just for the sake of diversity is also a form of perversity. Ms. Merkel has made it clear that some immigrants are demonstratively more worthy of inviting into Germany than others. More than that, she wants to welcome into Germany skilled people with strong track records. That is the kind of sound policy toward immigration America must adopt if America is to remain strong.

WHITE MALE INVENTIONS

Trains, planes, cars, rockets, telescopes, tires, telephones, radios, television, electricity, atomic energy, computers, and fax machines. All miracles made possible by the minds and spirits of men with names like Ampere, Bell, Caselli, Edison, Ohm, Faraday, Einstein, Fleming, Cohen, Teller, Shockley, Hertz, Marconi, Morse, Popov, Ford, Volta, Michelin, Dunlop, Watt, Diesel, Galileo, and other "dead white males."

What I'm about to say is tantamount to blasphemy in this politically correct day and age; yet truth is truth. How long are we going to pretend that origins play no role in our world, the origins of the inventions, science, technology, and economics of the world in which we live?

Our present society owes much to the revolution in electronics and computer technology. But saying this is not enough, for these things didn't just spring into existence by themselves. They have traceable origins. It's no mystery. Just look at the list of names in your history books and their national origins.

The great majority of advancements past and present have been brought about by the genius and inventiveness of that most "despicable" of colors and genders, the dreaded white male, or, to be exact, by specific, individual white males. This is not to discredit the many contributions coming from nonwhites, but fact is fact. Our most important and consequential inventions have come almost exclusively from white males.

Curse me, or all white males, if you wish; that changes nothing. But if you call me a liar, you'll have to come up with the proof that I'm wrong. Remember, I didn't say there were no important contributions by nonwhites; I said the *great majority*. Of course, I know about such things as the Chinese and gunpowder, but they didn't take it much beyond firecrackers and pyrotechnics. And I know about the pyramids and masonry of South America and the zero of the Arabs.

Would we have atomic physics and electricity if it hadn't been for the ancient Greek philosophers who, for example, had the idea that all matter consists of tiny atoms? Aristotle (Fifth Century BC, Twenty-Fifth Century pre-P.C.) used electric charges to treat gout. Archimedes perceived the center of gravity of solids, cylinders, and spheres, and Greek physicians made tremendous advancements in medicine.

From the basic discoveries of Greek civilization it went to the Romans, and after the fall of Rome it passed to later Europeans who expanded on this scientific knowledge. In modern times these ideas were developed by such men as Volta, Ampere, Watt, Bell, Edison, and Einstein, who provided the basis for most of the technical wonders of today.

All of them dreaded white males.

Maybe you got your enlightenment from one of the Ivy League institutions of dis-education. Maybe they taught you that it's all the result of white racism and oppression. That every time a potential Einstein, Edison, or Ford popped up in the Third World, a white hit squad would swoop down and eliminate him before he had a chance to prove himself. Or maybe their schools refused to teach him in the Ebonics of his day. Or maybe they didn't have proper day care facilities. Or maybe our would-be innovator came from a "dysfunctional family."

But the facts tell us that many of the great men pursued their genius at great personal risk—like the astronomer Galileo, who proved that the earth revolves around the sun. He and other men of genius and courage refused to be suppressed even if it meant their lives. They would permit no race, gender, group, or class to keep them from their pursuit of truth and excellence, whatever the cost.

If you eliminate, suppress, or debase the white male, you kill the goose that laid the golden egg. If you ace him out with "affirmative" action, exile him from the family, teach him that he's a blight on mankind, then bon voyage to our society. We will devolve into a Third World cesspool. Where has there ever before in history been a group of human beings who have brought about the likes of the Magna Carta, the U.S. Constitution, and the countless life-saving and life-improving inventions that we now enjoy?

Now it is certainly true that China did lead the world in technology and commercial inventiveness about one thousand years ago. They had great coal-mining operations, gunpowder, six-masted sailing ships, and intense commercial enterprise. But it all collapsed because the elites, the long-nailed mandarins, centralized control—a thousand years before Mao—and crushed the expansion and inventions.

Does this mean we should sit back and let ourselves be governed by someone just because he's a white male? Of course it doesn't. It means simply that we shouldn't suppress anyone, including white males. Let our God-given gifts run free in a free and just society, free from the oppression and tyranny of social engineers. If anyone has gifts beyond our own—be he a white male or any other—be grateful.

Maybe we have gifts that in some small way can contribute something of value as well. One way or another, we're all in the same boat. Few of us have truly outstanding gifts. And most of us have to humbly accept that there are others around who are more gifted than we are. In a Democratic society, it's not for Big Brother to decide who shall thrive and who shall struggle in the hive.

Do you see what's happening? The liberals have turned the issue of immigration into a matter of the "Fairness Police." We need, they claim, to let everybody in—it's only fair. Why turn away some and not others? Once they're here, the liberals use affirmative action to advance people not on the basis of their skills, abilities, or achievements, but on their skin color.

Watch where this sideways thinking has brought us. The Fairness Police are knocking on the door of . . . video game manufacturers.

VIDEO GAMES AREN'T DIVERSE ENOUGH

Headline: "Video Games Not Diverse Enough."

Whether you care to believe it or not, someone actually studied video games and found out there are too many white males playing the lead characters. Where did this nonsense come from? I'm telling you, these liberals have too much time on their hands.

According to the article, today's video games provide very little racial and gender diversity. This is breaking my heart. The study claims that virtually all the heroes are white males "with women representing just 16 percent of human characters." Well, so what? That's what the kids want. What are you people—nuts?

"Nearly all the game heroes are white males." Well, maybe we could put some Arab males in the video games. Maybe we could dress some in flowing robes or maybe in dirty nightshirts. That way we could be sure to have some diversity in video games.

Maybe we could have some women who look like Rosie O'Donnell. You know, with a strap-on chin. Yea, have a strap-on chin to make them look more like a male. Eighty-six percent of black women were portrayed as victims of violence, and there were no Hispanic female characters. How racist. How racist!

The study also said that 89 percent of the games contained some violent content. Of course, that's why the kids buy them. Half of which resulted in damage to a game character. Don't these idiots understand that that's how the kids get it out of their system? When I was a kid, I wanted cap guns. I shot everyone who came in my little apartment.

I remember I had cap guns, and I dressed up as one of my cowboy heroes. I don't recall who he was. And anyone who came in our little apartment—my father's friends, my mother's friends—I would shoot them with my cap guns.

I've never shot anyone since with a real gun.

Never killed anybody.

I had a Daisy BB gun. I was always impressed with weapons.

Despite the fact that I was on the high school rifle team, I never killed a soul. I never picked up the gun and ran through the halls. I never ran amok and shot anybody. I got it out of my system with a cap gun. Don't these morons understand that?

Boys want to be tough. Boys want to be heroes. They don't want to grow up with a dress. They don't want to wear a garter belt and stockings in school.

Why am I surprised that the lefties want more diversity and perversity in video games? I say, go ahead and create one. See if there's a market for it. Put out a video game with a diverse character and see if it sells.

It's a free market.

What the rad-libs want is for the government to fund "diverse video games" and then force the little video veggies to play them. In other words, they want socialism. Do you finally understand what socialism is? It's the imposition of unwanted thoughts and services on people. It's the imposition of broken products on people.

The next thing the left will attempt to mandate will be free video games for the illegal immigrants to play before they sneak across the border. The INS will be required to provide a "Border-Buster," batteries included, as a door prize.

KFC AND THE AMERICAN DREAM

Sometimes I'd rather go to Kentucky Fried Chicken and eat at the buffet line with the Mexicans than go to the pretentious restaurants in San Fransicko. I'm sick of the waiters with open running sores on their faces, with earrings, hovering all around me when I eat. I get tired of dining next to inane fools at the adjacent table as they sit there with bland faces looking like uncured beef in a suit.

The other day, I went to Kentucky Fried Chicken—$6.95, all you can eat. I'm not ashamed to tell you, I had the best lunch I'd had in years. What a meal! Just a little side note: if you peel off the skin, KFC has the moistest chicken in the world. It's unbelievable.

So I went and sat in the back in the dining room. I noticed that was where all the poorest of the poor Mexican folks ate. They were there with their wives and their children, probably on their day off. I was the only "white" guy in the place. Anyway, I start knocking down the chicken. I start on the mashed potatoes and the fresh green beans and the carrots, all boiled. It was delicious.

While I ate, I watched a Mexican guy with his wife and maybe four or five kids. He was a man who loved his children. I watched as his daughter laughed and played. I saw the father as he picked her up and kissed her on the face. I saw the joy as they talked to each other. I thought, "I haven't seen love like that in so long." It was unbelievable.

The last time I'd seen a love like that was when I was a little child and my father kissed my sister or me on the face. Because he, too, was an immigrant. That's the last time I saw an expression of love come from a father to a daughter like that from that Mexican guy in the KFC.

As I watched this father hugging his kids, I thought, *Man, this is what we're fighting for. We're working to preserve the freedom that enables a family to play and love each other without fear of being harmed.* Which is why we must do everything in our power— including racial profiling as needed—to scrub out those who are here, right now, waiting to snuff out the American Dream.

WHEN LEGAL IMMIGRATION ROCKS THE BOAT

A day in October, 2002, will go down as one of the bleakest days in recent memory for me. I watched in stunned amazement as a member of the administration, his tone nonchalant, pronounced, "The prospects of a future attack against the United States are almost certain. I'd like to be able to say it's never going to happen again, but I don't believe anybody who has looked at it can say that. We don't know if it's going to be tomorrow, next week, or next year."

As I listened to him, I wanted to scream—or break something.

The government's job is to protect the people.

Now they're telling us they cannot protect the people.

We can expect to be killed any day. And we can't do anything about it. What should I do, sit here and say that he's right? Am I the only one who hears the doublespeak?

We don't have bunkers to run to. We don't have air-raid sirens to warn us of an enemy attack. We don't have airplanes to whisk us away in the event of an emergency. But, according to our leaders, we're supposed to get back to business as usual . . . just remember, a terrorist attack could happen any day, anywhere, anytime . . . but get back to normal.

Let me decode the doublespeak.

Our leaders tell us, "You know what, you little sheeple? Just keep popping your Prozac. Keep working and paying your taxes. If you get killed or come home in a body bag from the mall, no problem. We'll just replace you with another mote in the mire. We've got plenty of ciphers to keep working, to keep plugging money into the system."

How are we Americans supposed to wake up every day, leave our families, go to work, come home, and repeat the drill day after day while our government makes bureaucratic statements with no connection to reality? I refuse to walk around with a bull's-eye painted on my forehead.

Do you understand the implications of these empty suits? Why is America waiting around for the terrorists to hurt us? What kind of schmuck government says, "Expect it," but there's little we can do to stop it?

The government says it can't protect us. What *can* they do?

Tax us? Charge us with a hate crime?

I'll tell you something. There *is* a way to prevent terrorism. It involves two components: racial profiling and closing our borders to all immigrants from terrorist-sponsoring nations. Do you get the picture? How obvious is that? It doesn't take a genius to figure out who's behind these potential future terrorist attacks. Or, do I need to spell it out for those of you on government-subsidized marijuana?

Let's start by ruling out who it might and might not be.

Just go down the list.

You wouldn't expect a terrorist to be a white, Irish nun, would you? How about an elderly man from England? Or, a Canadian figure skater? Make your list. Guess who'll be at the top?

Middle Eastern men. Yes, men of Arab ancestry.

Why should we "discriminate" against them? Because nineteen out of nineteen of the terrorists—those scum who cut the throats of our women, who smashed planes into buildings killing thousands of us—were Middle Eastern males. *Memo to the CIA:* That's a clue. That detail is a fairly strong indication of where we might focus our efforts to prevent another bloodbath.

That's how racial profiling works.

But the left has diluted our war against terrorism by twisting it until it now resembles the diversity of a McDonald's commercial. The left has created an atmosphere where politicians are afraid of the pinkos at the *New York Times* and the *Washington Post*. They're afraid of being accused of intolerance and then losing twelve voters.

We know where the people are. But we won't go get them.

The radicals on the left will put us in jail for the sin of racial profiling faster than they would a potential bomber. That's how garbled our thinking has become.

The country is finished when the "top" leaders say we're gonna get blown up, somewhere, somehow—maybe in an apartment building—but that there's no way to stop it. They release a general warning to apartment managers, but they don't tell you who to look for.

Uh, Mr. Liberal, it would be helpful to know if there is a particular ethnicity we should be looking for in this apartment building threat. They won't tell us. They're just giving us another "warning" to cover their behinds.

Take the nutcases in the media. These journalists seem more preoccupied with their pancake makeup than the fact terrorists plan to level entire cities. Their off-the-cuff commentaries on fighting terrorists sound like this:

> If you see a nun in her eighties, with blonde hair and blue eyes, be sure to report her. She could be harboring a molesting priest. However, if you see a suspicious person of Middle Eastern decent, and you were to report him, you are liable to be guilty of a hate crime. You are liable to be investigated by the IRS, INS, CBS, ABC, NBC, FBI, CIA, or one of the other alphabet groups because you may have committed a race crime.

It's time to take the powers of government and turn them against the people who want to harm us. It's time we took the gloves off and went after them where they're hiding.

Do I have to spell it out for you? Fine. I'll do it for free. You don't even need to hire a consultant. Here's how we defend ourselves. Case in point. Recently, fifty men, all of Middle Eastern descent—none were blonde nuns from Ireland—snuck into the country on a ship. Where do you think a Middle Eastern terrorist waiting to strike would go to hide?

I'll give you four choices.

a. He'd hide among white Irish nuns.

b. He'd hide among albino mental cases.

c. He'd hide among orthodox Jews.

d. He'd hide in another unnamed community.

How about "d"?

Would that be good police work? Can we agree on that? Fine. Then you send out the FBI and the police and you knock on every door. Do you have any visitors? Did anyone bring any strange packages? Who's in the back room? We don't care, we're coming in. Shake them down. Toss the pillows around. You'll find something or someone hiding in one of the closets. They're swimming like fish in the ethnic communities where they blend in.

How come I know this and the "intelligence community" hasn't figured it out? Or, if they've figured it out, why aren't they acting on it? What are they afraid of?

A critical editorial from the *New York Times*?

When the next Red Diaper Doper Baby stands up and protests, I say throw him in a dark cell until this is over. You liberals should drop dead for what you've done to my country. You should get a stroke for what you've done to our ability to defend ourselves—you rotten, stinking RDDB lawyers who have raped our country. Traitors, all of you!

You have tied the hands of the people in this country who want to live because you are death worshipers, you liberals. Drugs, sex, and rock 'n' roll.

Then there are the handful of callers to my nationally syndicated radio program who tell me all this terrorism against America would be stopped if America just backed away from Israel. They say, let the Jews be exterminated. Then what? Do you think we'll have happy little Arabs dancing around, thrilled that Israel is gone? You think then they'll leave America alone? That's the position of ignorant bigots who only know what to think by reading their Nazi brochure that arrived over the weekend.

Abandoning Israel is another wicked lie promoted by the left. Does Israel's existence explain the Muslim war against India, Indonesia, or the Philippines?

To stop terrorism, I'd suggest the FBI go to the worst gangs in

America and find the baddest blacks, whites, Hispanics, and Asians and then bring them into the inner sanctum, into the president's cabinet. I'd say, "Look, boys, here's our situation. We're at war with these terrorists. Tell us, how would you stop it?" I guarantee you they'd solve it much faster than these frat boys in Washington.

My suggestion isn't a new idea. It's been done before, during World War II. The government of elitists knew there was a problem on the waterfronts of America. They knew the Germans had Gestapo spies all over the East and the West Coasts. They also knew who controlled the waterfront—the Mafia.

Back then, they went to Lucky Lucciano and cut a deal with the Mafia. The Mafia made sure the Nazis didn't function on the waterfront. Period. End of story. If a spy was found, he'd get a meat hook in the back and end up swimming with the fishes.

Call it Long Shore Justice.

That was the end of 99 percent of the Nazis on the waterfront.

It's been done before. It must be done again, or we're all cooked. Today, our leaders hire smart idiots from Harvard and Yale to analyze the situation. I say it's time to stop with the frat-boy talk.

There. I gave you the brass tacks.

Solution One: Go to the baddest Americans and bring them to the seats of power and ask *them* what to do. Gangsters love capitalism. They hate socialism; they hate terrorism. Why? It's bad for their business.

Solution Two: We've got nuclear subs. These subs are loaded to the hatches with nuclear warheads that can be targeted to within a centimeter of Saddam's mustache. The president should tell that terrorist, "So much as one hair of one child gets singed, there will be no Baghdad. One American child is worth more than your entire rotten, stinking city. You let one kid die, Saddam, and Baghdad is toast."

You think that's a little harsh, think Hiroshima and Nagasaki. Back then, much better men realized *it's us vs. them*. They declared

146

war on America. President Truman didn't want to sacrifice five hundred thousand or a million more American boys.

Here comes the bomb.

Here comes the judge.

That was the end of World War II.

But today, we're being told, "No, you expect to die."

And when more Americans die, the politicians will line up to get on with Larry Seltzer, who, leaning forward in his chair with his suspenders, will ask, "So, can you predict the next terrorist attack?"

Joe Politician will say, "Well, Larry, if you remember back on blah, blah, blah, I warned America there most certainly would be future attacks."

"Yes, that was very good. How about today? Can you give us any advance warning now?"

"Yes, Larry. We can expect another attack. We don't know where. We don't know when. Um, and there's nothing we can do about it. But, Larry, if the terrorists tell us where and when, we'll certainly take that under consideration."

What does this have to do with immigration?

Everything.

As I've said, a country is defined by her borders, language, and culture. Take our borders. Each time we admit someone from a country identified as a beehive of terrorism, we flirt with disaster. The president should issue an executive order that *slams shut* our borders to all immigration petitions, all student visas, and all tourism requests from Iraq, Iran, the Sudan, and any Krapistan that is on our list of terrorist nations.

How many body bags will it take before our leaders take decisive action and do the obvious?

8

DANCING ON THE CULTURAL ABYSS:

Red Diaper Doper Babies Rule!

⌒

I THINK IT WAS FRIDAY NIGHT. A friend of mine invited me to dinner. We went to a place I'd been to before, a French restaurant. I remember I ordered the tuna. I don't mean a tuna sandwich on toast. That's what I eat every morning. I ordered the ahi tuna. Fine.

The waitress at this would-be "cool" French restaurant came back to the table and asked me how I'd like the tuna cooked. I told her I'd like it well done. I don't want it pink in the middle. I don't eat blood on my fish. I'm not like the old man in the sea in a boat, you know, with my knuckles bleeding.

She gave me that raised-eyebrow look as she scribbled a note on her pad. She turned and headed for the kitchen. I could guess what she was thinking. I thought, but didn't say, *You got fire back there? The restaurant should cook the blasted thing. I don't want raw fish. If I wanted raw fish, what do I need a French restaurant for? Use your fire and cook the fish.*

After a few moments, she came back and told me, "The chef says ahi is far too delicate to cook all the way through. It has to be pink in the middle."

I started to boil.

The running joke with me is that there's not a single restaurant left in San Francisco I can go into without the risk of being poisoned because I happen to like my food cooked the way I like it—and I say so. I may start taking a food taster with me in case they put arsenic in my onion soup.

Anyway, when the fish came I knew we were headed for trouble. The thing was barely cooked. I ate it anyway because it's all I wanted, and I was hungry. At the end of the meal, the waitress had the nerve to ask, "How was the ahi?"

What do you expect from me? I gave her a Savage answer.

"How was the ahi? With the pink middle? With blood running out of it like the hook just came out of the fish's guts?" I said, "I really like Japanese food; that was quite good. I really enjoyed the sushi." I could see my friend's face turning red as if to say, "Oh, there he goes again."

Then I added, "By the way, you can tell the chef the next time he wants to dictate how I'm going to eat his fish, he can pay for it. But while I'm paying $28 for a piece of fish worth $3 maybe he can cook it the way I want it." I said it nicely, I wasn't nasty, and I'm still going to place an "x" through that phony restaurant with bad wine.

What attitudes they have in these liberal cities—imagine the nerve? *You're* paying and *he's* telling you how you have to eat his fish. I guess I shouldn't be surprised.

That's the way liberalism works.

We're told what to think.

We're told what we'll like.

We're told how to eat, act, think, and live by others who supposedly know what's best for us.

When it comes to our culture, we're being told by the liberals to let the illegal invaders as well as the legal newcomers redefine and reshape our culture into *their* image. The liberals have got it completely backward.

Why is that such a big deal? Because our *culture* is what defines *the heart and soul* of America.

Do you understand what I'm saying to you? Or has your mind become dull from staring at too much TV?

You and I have been handed something of incredible value (this great country) that others (our forefathers) fought to establish against extreme odds. Many of these brave men and women gave their lives for the freedoms we now enjoy. And many more, even today, are dying to protect us.

I don't know about you, but I refuse to allow the liberals to redefine America's greatness by diluting her culture. Look at our two-hundred-year history. You'll find what makes America great: We are a nation populated with pioneers, dreamers, inventors, leaders, opportunity makers, builders, thinkers, poets, artists, musicians, doctors, and scientists. I could go on and on.

Is it any wonder, then, that today America has led the world in technology, medicine, science, and space exploration? Our freedom, coupled with the entrepreneurial spirit and the incentive capitalism brings, has produced these many advances and breakthroughs. Not to mention that we enjoy the highest standard of living anywhere on the planet.

Now, look at the other nations of the world.

You won't find these advances and breakthroughs in socialist countries. You won't find individuals working hard to excel, to dream, and to build a brighter future in countries where the self-serving socialist government hands the people a loaf of bread and a blanket while telling them which government agency they must work in.

As I said earlier, America has been richly blessed.

America has had a glorious past.

America is now facing a cultural crossroad. Why?

America is caught in the crosshairs of those who hate this land, hate what we stand for, and hate what we've accomplished. Her people have been sold down the river by the socialist liberals who worship at the altar of secular humanism and multi-culti-ism.

For the better part of two hundred years, America was known as the "melting pot." In the past, that meant when immigrants came to our country *they assimilated the dominant cultural experience.* They immediately learned the native tongue (that's English—in case your hat is on backward and you forgot). They worked hard to fit in, and they wanted to make a contribution to the greater societal good. The result?

America became a country that benefited from the blending of the best of all immigrant cultures. We are Americans first and foremost. That's the miracle:

We're a diverse people with a shared freedom.

We represent a variety of nationalities but are one nation.

We have a range of skills but a shared opportunity to excel.

We have many voices but one tongue.

We live in individual states but ultimately in one united country. And for almost two centuries this experiment in democracy has been the envy of the world. Even so, these achievements were not good enough for the psychotic left. These deranged individuals, who obviously suffer from a deficiency of vitamin B3, have spent the last forty years recasting "America, the Melting Pot" as "America, the Multi-Culti-Pot."

How did they do it?

By accusing you of collective guilt. They claimed you and I were oppressing and abusing (fill in the blank). We oppress the gays, blacks, Latinos, Asians, Indians, plants, bugs, minerals, the ozone, the snail darter, the wetlands, and the moon. The left figured out long ago that *social chaos* is a wonderful tool to help them usher in their socialist worldview.

Having labeled us as intolerant cavemen, their solution has been to sell *multiculturalism* as a good, even a preferred social construct to *nationalism*.

What does this mean?

With multiculturalism, immigrants *don't* attempt to assimilate the dominant culture. Instead, they retain their distinct cultural heritage. They don't bother to learn English, choosing to speak their own language and then demand that we print ballots in eighteen languages. And, in the spirit of multiculturalism, they'll sue you in a heartbeat if you don't acquiesce to their ethnic sensitivities.

Multiculturalism has castrated America's dominant cultural identity and, instead, has imposed the culture of the immigrant's "country of origin" on us. Where will multiculturalism take us if left unchecked? I'll connect the dots:

1. America the melting pot
2. America the multi-culti pot
3. America the chamber pot

As you well know, a chamber pot holds nothing of value and nothing worth preserving. So once the sheeple come to view America as a chamber pot, they won't have a sense of national identity. They will have no sense of national unity. No sense of national pride. No sense of responsibility. No national honor.

Ultimately, "America the Chamber Pot" puts this country on the "pathway to apathy and anarchy"—and that, as the liberals know, is the perfect climate in which to reap the fruits of socialism. Pushing us farther along that pathway to apathy and anarchy is the attack by the left upon the cultural backbone of the nation.

WEIMAR, ONCE AGAIN

America is now living through the equivalent social chaos that the Germans experienced in the Weimar Republic in pre-Hitler

Germany before 1933. Like cancer, on the Democrat side, we have the same diseased radical political leadership infecting all levels of government. These carcinogenic cells cater to pornographers, drug dealers, perverts, foreign immigrants, and foreign competitors. These leaders disdain church, family, fathers, mothers, children, and decency.

Believe me, and as recent history has demonstrated, there is no essential difference between the Democrats and the leadership of the Weimar Republic. They share the same mentality. For years, the same disturbed mind-set has come back to haunt us again.

In the Democrat's America, Justice is not only blindfolded, she has been bound and prostituted. Justice has become a perverted masquerade where those in power are innocent even when proven guilty and where average Americans are guilty—with no money to prove their innocence. Their rights are mocked, and their values are the brunt of filthy humor.

When this kind of disease appears on earth, nature usually follows it by the opposite. When the world collapses this way, what happens? What inevitably follows this kind of decadence? Simply that, at some point, anarchy and social decay are followed by tyranny and oppression, as they were in Weimar Germany.

But, unlike Weimar, today we delude ourselves by thinking it can't happen in America.

A leading Democrat recently claimed before a radical "gay" group that the greatest problem today is hatred. But he himself is the source of this hatred. He and the others have done more than anyone to promulgate hostility and division among the groups of our society. They push hatred, envy, and suspicion wherever they go, while feigning compassion and understanding.

The truth is, the Demoncats are still up to their politics of personal destruction. Behind the smiles, finger wagging, and promises, there are only arrogance, corruption, and deceit.

Need we follow? Wasn't one Weimar enough?

In addition to the perversion of justice and the attack upon our cherished institutions of faith and family, these liberals stoke the flames of cultural chaos with their refusal to establish the recognition of English as the official language of the United States.

We're told:

> If you speak three languages, you're trilingual.
>
> If you speak two languages, you're bilingual.
>
> If you speak one language, you're an American.

Can't you see that these social engineers are insulting you? They collectively stick their pious noses in the air as they lecture the American people about the deficiency of speaking *just one language*. Once again, *you* are the problem. Come to think of it, your narrow-mindedness and your refusal to learn the language of the immigrant popu-lation approach the level of a hate crime.

Listen, sheeple, wake up before rigor mortis sets in!

Americans have been speaking English since the time of the Pilgrims. One language allows us to work together, to pull in the same direction, and to communicate effectively with one another. Progress stops when people can't communicate with each other. Ever hear of the biblical account of the Tower of Babel? Go read it sometime (Gen. 11:1–9) and you'll see that anyone who insists several languages are better than one is wrong. In fact, every current study has shown that children who are immersed in the English language when they come to America do better in school.

What about the notion of becoming well-rounded?

I know all about the well-rounded leftists we have in the country. I'm sure many of them are bisexual and bilingual at the same time. I'm sure that helps them greatly in their social life but not necessarily in their commercial life, nor in their educational progress. You can be trilingual, you can be multilingual, you can eat tongue, you can use your tongue, but the fact of the matter is that if you immerse children in English when they come here, they do much better in life than if you let them learn their native language.

If you fail to teach immigrants English, what they wind up becoming is either a maid at Motel 6, a grape-picker, or one of the leaf-blower people for the rest of their lives. It's the sure road to serf-dom. In fact, that is precisely why the liberals push bilingualism.

Socialists need a slave class.

PLATO'S *REPUBLIC*

As a teenager, I attended a city high school in New York. Back then, our required reading included classical literature and the writings of the Greek philosopher Plato. Today, Plato, Aristotle, and Shakespeare have been replaced by contemporary liberal works such as *Heather Has Two Mommies*, *Daddy's Roommate*, and Al Gore's *Earth in the Balance*.

This seismic shift in education is not an accident.

It's a core strategy of liberalism.

The libs know if they can inculcate young minds with their view of the world, they can change the direction of the American culture in as little as one generation. Aristotle said it best: "All who have meditated on the art of governing mankind are convinced that the fate of empires depends on the education of youth."

Before I get to Plato, there's something you should know about the Greeks. The Greeks had no Bible. What the Bible is to you or has been to us as a source of theology and morals, the poets were to the Greeks. Even without a Bible, morals were nevertheless involved in every discussion in ancient Greece.

Even Hillary Clinton cannot blame the Christian right for the fact that the ancient Greeks, who revered poetry and mythology, observed a moral code and explored theology. They openly discussed morality. They debated it. But in America, anyone who claims to be moral is considered a bigot. That's because you've been reeducated by the left. That's also why the liberals have worked so hard to domi-nate our schools and our universities.

In Plato's *Republic*, the philosopher warns of this brainwashing of youth. In classic Greek fashion, he first asks a question:

> Shall we just carelessly allow children to hear any casual tales which may be devised by casual persons, and to receive into their minds ideas for the most part the very opposite of those which we should wish them to have when they are grown up?

Reread his question and substitute the word *liberal* for the word *casual*. You'll understand why Plato answers his own question this way:

> We cannot . . . Anything received into the mind at that age is likely to become indelible and unalterable; and therefore it is most important that the tales which the young first hear should be mod-els of virtuous thoughts. There can be no nobler training than that.

Every society decides what is suitable for children, what is beneficial for children, what is for their well-being, what is good, and what is evil. In other words, Plato was encouraging fellow Greeks to exer-cise sort of an intellectual V-chip to prevent the telling of tales by "casual persons."

Plato understood that a distinction could and should be made between lies and "models of virtuous thoughts."

Today, the Commu-Nazis in the liberally dominated education system resist such distinctions for fear that their socialist agenda would be exposed for what it is: a fraud. A dangerous lie. Pure social-ist propaganda. And a radical grab to redefine the American culture.

I realize logic has been replaced by "feelings" in most of the world today. America, led by the liberal reeducation of young people, is moving back to a sort of new paganism—yes, almost a form of witchcraft—as the norm instead of the church. If we continue to move in that direction, we're going to repeat mistakes that will destroy America.

A FISH STORY

I'll give you the perfect example of what happens when liberals brainwash the sheeple with their stories, lies, and fabrications. It's a fish story, but it's true. A number of years ago, I went to a Chinese restaurant with another person. I won't mention her name because I don't want to embarrass her.

This particular restaurant had a fish tank filled with live fish, where the customer picked out the fish she wanted to eat. The waiter would come out with a net. He'd stick it in and pull out the fish you wanted, cook it, and then you'd eat it. Most people paid no attention to it.

I was sitting with my back to the tank. I don't remember what I ordered, but it wasn't fish. The person I was with didn't order fish, either. Throughout our meal, she kept looking over my shoulder at the fish tank. All of a sudden, she broke out in tears that wouldn't stop. I handed her a napkin and asked what was wrong. You know, I'm thinking maybe she ordered something a little too spicy.

She managed to say, "No. The fish . . . they're going to die. They're all gonna die!" She just wouldn't stop, she wouldn't let it go. I figured some liberal save-the-whale nutcase probably traumatized her back in kindergarten with the story of *Free Willy*, and now she was having a panic attack. Or at least an attack of conscience that *something* must be done.

You know what I had to do? I had to buy all the fish in the tank. I put them in buckets and took them down to San Francisco Bay to "release" them in the water. It's a true story. You don't have to believe it. I did it.

Now, a sane person would know that was a foolish thing for me to do. In fact, in a sane society, I'd be in a straitjacket for what I did. Why? Not all the fish were from the San Francisco Bay, and I'm sure predators ate them shortly thereafter. But to a brainwashed liberal, we had to save the fish. (Of course, you never see that kind of emotional concern from liberals when it comes to saving unborn children who are "all going to die.")

If liberalism prevails in this culture, a mosquito will become a protected species under hate-crime legislation. Sadly, evidence that the mental disease of liberalism is spreading is everywhere. Especially in the arena of the arts.

"DUNGISM," THE NEW ART SCHOOL OF THE IRRELIGIOUS LEFT

Impressionism, Cubism, Dadaism . . . and now the elites give us Dungism. Unlike the art school of Dadaism, which, despite the "dada" part of the word, has nothing to do with fathers, or "daddies," the new art school of Dungism—for that's what I call it—*does* have to do with dung.

Of course, the "dung" in Dungism can refer to actual excrement applied in such works of art (anti-art), or it can refer to any other sordid and depraved object one might choose to apply to an otherwise hallowed subject matter. And this, we are told by our liberal Dungists, is protected by the First Amendment to the Constitution—even when displayed in public institutions, which are supposed to remain free of religious, including antireligious, bias.

According to Dungism, it's okay to display a crucifix in public—as long as it's immersed in urine. Or the disgraceful depiction of the Virgin Mary—decorated with elephant excrement and porno clips of vaginas—displayed in the Brooklyn Museum of Art.

Let me tell you, I'm not going to bow to this school of art, nor to its twisting of the Constitution. They will not rub our faces in their filth and get away with it; I guarantee you that. There will be a verbal holy war. A new verbal crusade. And, sooner or later, it's coming to a neighborhood near you. Be sure of it.

The left and the decadent are very clever at twisting words to their own advantage. We know that. They debase the Catholic religion with their Dungistic "art" and call it freedom of speech. If they get away with it now, they will move on to the Protestants, Jews, and Muslims.

Even the Muslim Koran respects the Virgin Mary.

What are Christians waiting for?

This is a very emotional topic with me. I'm going to march with the Catholics even though I'm not a Catholic. And I'd wear a Catholic rosary to show my opposition to this abomination, proudly premiered in the Brooklyn Museum. Museums are supposed to preserve the objective history and culture of our nation and the world. But with liberalism driving the train, museums are becoming tools of a socialist propaganda to move us toward a totalitarian, one-world order.

Next they might show Torah scrolls or the Muslim Koran covered with manure. It's all part of the scheme to debase and destroy religious faith and replace it with the idol of global totalitarianism.

What gets me is the mad rush by the National Endowment of the Arts to be the official sponsor of Dungism. The government takes your tax dollars and then underwrites "artists" whose only agenda is to mock our values and debase our culture.

It's bad enough that our taxes are being used at all to support the arts. At least it wouldn't be so painful if the NEA were getting behind an artist of Beethoven's caliber.

I remember listening to Beethoven in the house. I had the music turned up real loud. I'm going to make an admission to you, and I'm not ashamed to admit it. Tears streamed from my eyes. Not because I was crying like a weepy, wimpy kind of thing. I was crying that God could create such beauty in the mind of a human being. I cannot comprehend how God could create a genetic combination that produces a Beethoven, compared to the filth and garbage in so much of today's pop music—or shown on television.

Actors make so much money with little talent, little brains. The degenerates that they glorify in Hollywood are unpardonable. Illiterate morons. They make millions and millions of dollars. All they do is stand up there on television, the empty skirts and empty suits, and read a script.

And liberals compare them to the talent of Beethoven?

When I listen to Beethoven, my body shudders. Why? Today, not only is mediocrity advanced, but the products of liberal Dungism are said to be worthy of a Grammy or whatever applicable award. Far be it from the sheeple to challenge Dungists on the basis of "good art" and "bad art."

What's more, if a ray of clear thinking were to pierce the fog in your mind and you, in turn, confronted Dungism on the grounds of "right and wrong," these self-absorbed, egocentric artists would just dismiss the question by echoing the liberal mantra: "*I don't believe in right and wrong. I believe in catch me if you can—there's no governing legal authority.*"

That's the new ethos of the day.

And it's destroying our culture.

Just look at what it's done to our legal system.

THE ACLU AND THE RED DIAPER DOPER BABIES

Are you beginning to understand why the radical left-wing agenda is so dangerous and why I've said extreme liberalism is a mental disease? I hope so, because if we don't reverse the spread of this cancerous growth, America will be cooked in a few short years.

If I had to point to the epicenter of this illiberal attack on our culture, it would have to be the hate-filled, socialist lawyers of the American Civil Liberties Union. These vultures have so picked apart the American legal system, American justice has been reduced to roadkill. All that remains of our courts is a rotting carcass of what was once the envy of the world.

Here, then, is the genesis of the RDDB.

You can see them everywhere. Just turn on your television. They usually have wild hair. Their eyes are usually bulging out. Usually, if you look very carefully, you will notice a slight white spittle at the corners of their mouths as their eyes bulge. It's typically more pronounced in the Harvard professors. Without question, they bulge and foam the most.

But I, as the original compassionate conservative, understand the condition. It's a result of their manic depression. I studied this in great detail. Apparently, the spittle could be controlled with a small dose of lithium. But once they put these Red Diaper Doper Baby lawyers from NYU on Prozac, the spittle started appearing again.

Today this unelected, largely invisible, secret society of RDDB lawyer-gangsters has waged a merciless war against America. Let us look at what the RDDBs of the ACLU, in its devious machinations, have done just recently.

The police in California enjoyed a unique protection for about seventeen years. A law, passed in 1982, allowed them to sue citizens who filed false complaints against them. I liked that law because most of the complaints against the police—most, not all—that I have followed are by paid activists who work for criminal enterprises and criminal businesses, seeking to throw out cases against drug dealers and their type. Of course, there are also those on the loony left who sue cops for a living.

The ACLU has successfully worked to strike down this law.

At the bidding of the ACLU, the Superior Court of San Francisco ruled against this law that protected the police from frivolous and malicious suits. Again we see that the courts in San Francisco are not so superior after all. Watching their antics is like watching the apes at the zoo mimic each other. There's no mistaking it; this is what the courts of San Francisco have become.

Some misguided souls think that the ACLU is there to protect freedom of speech and the Constitution. But I tell you that anything that falls outside its leftopathic agenda is, as far as it's concerned, also outside the protection of "freedom of speech" and the Constitution.

The Founding Fathers, in their infinite wisdom, crafted the greatest document for mankind's liberation in the history of the world; it's called the Constitution of the United States of America. The RDDBs who use the ACLU as a support group, continue to work to rip this hallowed document to pieces a thousand different ways and a thousand different times.

Of course, whenever it suits the RDDBs, they wrap themselves in the Constitution and the flag.

Does anyone really think it's the ACLU that keeps people like me from being thrown in jail, as might happen in China, for speaking out like this? Anyone with any sense knows the ACLU and the RDDBs would bring China right into our very homes if we would let them. And they would jump for joy to see people like me put away for good. That's how dedicated the ACLU is to liberty and justice.

Another example is in order. In California, the people voted via popular initiative to turn back the "invasion from Mexico and China." They voted to stop giving education and medicine to illegal aliens.

The ACLU shopped this popular state initiative to a radical, left-wing federal judge, and managed to trash the votes of nearly six million Californians, condemning our public schools and health care systems to a Third World existence. The capo of the Los Angeles "family" of the ACLU actually celebrated this blow against the people!

So who are these ACLU fiends?

If we focus on them as individuals, we find most were brought up in dysfunctional homes, by commie parents, and attended commie camps in the summer. They're a psychotic bunch of Red Diaper Doper Babies who were suckled on Karl Marx. I'm sure that many are *non compos mentis* and survive on medication, yet they are quite affluent due to the enormous settlements they extort with bogus lawsuits while they pose as champions of the downtrodden!

The truth is that they are beasts of prey living off the downtrodden, and they are responsible for much of the lack of justice in our society and for the perpetuation of our social problems.

America cries out for a strong leader to arise, disband, defund, and depose these lawyer-gangsters before we all end up in a new, Rwanda-like reality. Do you think that's an overstatement? Watch how the ACLU-Nazi thought police want to control your speech and your freedoms.

JESUS SAVES? NOT IF THE ACLU CAN HELP IT

The ACLU-Gestapo filed a federal lawsuit against a small town in southeastern Louisiana. Why? These ACLU-RDDB kooks wanted the good citizens of Franklinton to take down a sign that proclaimed: "Jesus is Lord over Franklinton."

Whatever happened to the notion of "community standards"? If the people of Franklinton don't have a problem with it, what business is it of the ACLU? The ACLU has such nerve. It's gone insane, over the edge. Its goons don't belong in America. They don't belong in this country.

The ACLU is attacking people who are good Christians. You don't have to be religious to respect Christianity any more than you have to be Muslim to respect a Muslim's right to pray five times a day. But you absolutely have to agree with me that the ACLU, in attacking religion in this country, is a demented, sick, negative force.

While the ACLU storm troopers were on a roll, they threatened to sue the mayor of Inglis, Florida, unless she removed a proclamation banning Satan within the town limits. You know what? You can find Satan in the town limits. Every time one of the boys from NYU drives through that town, you can see Satan sitting in the car.

Just as the Taliban cloaked themselves in the religion of Islam, the ACLU cloaks itself in the false premise that it speaks for the First Amendment. It's the exact same terrorism! The ACLU is an enemy of the American people. It is an enemy of the American way. Does that sound harsh?

Just months after the September 11 terrorist attacks, the ACLU printed and distributed a pamphlet in seven languages telling men how to legally avoid answering police who are conducting dragnets for individuals who may be in the country to disperse nuclear, chemical, and biological weapons. Tell me, whose side are these people on? This is the last straw as far as I'm concerned.

These so-called civil liberties groups are the ones to look into for aiding and abetting the enemy. You can bust them on RICO statutes for conspiracy to conduct a criminal enterprise.

CESSPOOL OF THE MIND

The same RDDBs who want to scrub out "Jesus" from welcome signs, who want to pull crosses off the walls of World War II memorials, are the same bunch whose saving grace, in their minds, would be to defend Osama bin Laden if given the chance.

A Harvard professor, in a mock defense on *Court TV*, actually submitted a sketch of how to defend OBL in court. The strategy? First, argue that OBL and al-Qaida did a lot of things, even good things. Next, to skirt racketeering charges, argue that al-Qaida was a holding company, not a corporation, with lots of independents operating on their own. Attorneys should also deny OBL's specific authorization for the particular attacks, though he may have taken credit for them afterward.

According to this leading liberal at Harvard—which is the primary training ground for many RDDBs—that's what the defense might argue. Let me decode his liberal gibberish. His approach would be the equivalent of arguing the following at the Nuremberg

165

trials of Hitler: "Yeah, well, you can't prove that Adolf Hitler dropped the Zyklon B on the Jews in the gas chambers. While we found the pellets, and while we know that Mr. Hitler was anti-Semitic, you can't prove beyond a reasonable doubt that Mr. Hitler in fact gassed the Jews. What happened to the Jewish people was horrendous. Admittedly."

The codefense lawyer from Princeton would then stand up and add, "And, Mr. Hitler may be an evil man. But that doesn't mean that we should trample on his constitutional rights. That doesn't mean that in our attempt to seek justice we should destroy the very system that permits us this justice. And that's why I say, ladies and gentlemen of the jury, you cannot prove beyond a reasonable doubt the guilt of Mr. Hitler. Mr. Hitler did not ever pull the switch. There's no picture of Hitler putting any Zyklon B in a gas chamber, ladies and gentlemen. And so I say, you must find Mr. Hitler innocent of the charges."

That's the dangerous mind of the radical left.

In the face of all common sense and decency, it continues to push these bedeviled opinions.

Take the constant warnings over terrorism in America. The officials of New York City have been rightly concerned about another attack. What did they do? They put in place a high-tech surveillance system that scrutinizes the faces of all tourists and guests who visit the Statue of Liberty. The face recognition technology compares each picture to a database of known offenders and terrorist suspects (provided by the FBI) at a rate of one million images a second.

Governor George Pataki was forced to defend his move when the ACLU protested! Pataki said, "People are still coming to New York City, to the Statue of Liberty, from around the country and around the world because they appreciate that this is a secure, safe, and free city."

What did the ACLU say about this antiterrorism tool? They charged it was "an insult to the American people." One leg-crosser spokeschick for the ACLU called the cameras a violation of civil rights and the right to privacy (both are pet peeves of all RDDBs). She was more concerned that the face-recognition technology would "only create an increased danger that individuals will be wrongly accused and harassed."

What about becoming wrongly blown up in a plane, moron?

She had the nerve to say, "One day, we'll wake up and find we have no privacy whatsoever."

At least she'd be able to wake up the next day if the cameras she's so opposed to prevented another explosion. Somebody buy her a clue. Even then, I'm not sure it would help. Sometimes the mental disease of liberalism is irreversible.

HATE CRIMES BECOMING FATE CRIMES

Thanks to the ACLU's terroristlike practices and policies, Americans must pass a newly created "hate crime" legal test. In the interest of fairness, I, Michael Savage, have combed the news stories and present the following cases for your consideration.

Not long ago, three police officers were ambushed by a gunman. The cops were responding to a 911 call. The police officers were white; the assailant was black. The gunman executed the police one after another. He shot himself after the arrival of backup officers who had him surrounded.

Was this a hate crime?

The media doesn't seem interested in finding out. If the police officers had been black and the assailant white, don't you think they might have looked into this possibility?

Not long before this tragic event, five Asian gang members brutally raped a white teenage girl as part of their gang initiation. They openly admitted to the police that they did it *because* she was white. Where was the media outrage at this admittedly race-motivated hate crime?

Just imagine the outcry if the girl had been Asian or black and the perpetrators had been young white punks. Is she, an innocent young girl, any less worthy of our concern than Matthew Shepard, the best-known homosexual who was beaten to death? Is the one any more or less a "hate" crime than the other?

The media turned Shepard into a virtual Christ figure, but the teenage girl and the slain police officers seem to be strangely missing from the headlines.

I wouldn't bring these incidents to your attention if they weren't among countless similar ones that have received next-to-zero media coverage. Could it be that some of this anti-white, anti-straight violence is provoked by media coverage that portrays whites, particularly hetero white males, as the cause of all race hatred and violence?

Could it be that this type of media bias is stirring up the very racial paranoia and hatred the ACLU and their type pretend to condemn? Might they be following an agenda of their own for a socialist, totalitarian America, initiated by vilifying white males and turning them into submissive wimps incapable of putting up a fight?

The answer is obvious, at least to any observant person. Anyone who thinks the media slant is just innocent liberalism, or a matter of giving the public what they want, is beneath moronic. But it's nothing new. The "Big Lie" and "divide and conquer" are as old as man himself. Just wait; next in line for social castration will be minority males as well.

HISTORY CHANNEL

I remember watching a film about the battle for Stalingrad. The Nazis were trying to crush Stalingrad. They lost one million German troops, thank God. But the Russians ended up sacrificing two million of their people to defend their city, which was ultimately reduced to rubble. As I watched, I couldn't imagine what this kind of deprivation would be like. To see people butchering each other,

burning farms—*tens of thousands of farms* burned to the ground by
the enemy.

People tortured.

People starving to death.

People freezing in the snow because the Nazis wanted to expand
their empire into Russia.

The thought struck me that in this country, thanks to the ACLU,
if someone doesn't serve water fast enough to a certain ethnic group
in Denny's, they lose forty-eight million dollars because there's a
greedy group of jackals with law degrees. Here, if someone sneezes
in a restaurant and someone thinks that they heard a racist statement in the sneeze, they win millions of dollars.

When you compare our civil rights "issues" to the real tragedies
of human history, it's embarrassing, a travesty. And I pray to God
that there's a special hell for radical lawyers.

I pray to God that the people who benefit from these phony
civil rights lawsuits will be castigated—if not in this life, then in the
next. I don't care if you have a fancy home and you think you're a
social butterfly. I don't care if you are an ethnic group who made
millions of dollars and bought yourself new houses and cars with
your winnings.

I pray to God that you will pay dearly for your deceitful lawsuits.

You are ruining America.

ARE JEWISH LIBERALS TO BLAME?

One tactic of the left is to pit groups of people against one another.
The libs paint with labels and broad generalizations, hoping to color
our opinions of each other.

So much for their celebration of multiculturalism.

Their goal? Divide and conquer the American sheeple.

I see evidence of this division and hostility on the rise from callers to my nationally syndicated radio program. These grumblings come from the average Joe who has clearly embraced the liberals' politics of personal destruction. In these grumblings, I hear the blood libel against the Jewish people that bubbled to the surface with killing consequences in Nazi Germany and elsewhere.

When talking about the demise of America, I increasingly get asked the question: *Are Jewish liberals to blame?*

Here's my answer: Have you ever met an Irish liberal? Have you ever met an African-American liberal? Have you ever encountered an Italian liberal? I have, and in each case I can provide examples of other races who, when they become overly identified with the radical cause, are equal to Marx and Engels.

To counter the question and the blood libel, I would pose the following question: Where would America's national defense be without the great Jewish minds of Einstein, Teller, and Cohen? Einstein, of course, gave us the Theory of Relativity; Edward Teller gave us the H-bomb; and Sam Cohen gave us the neutron bomb.

Therefore, the question about Jewish liberals has no meaning.

At times, the most vocal voices the media turn to when they want to denigrate God, country, family and apple pie come inordinately from one race or the other. However, on balance, there are plenty of Sharptons, Daschles, Kennedys, and others to make the liberal coalition quite a rainbow. A rainbow of just one hue—red.

DO BLACKS OWE JEWS REPARATIONS?

The Third Wave leftist hoaxsters are pushing "reparations" for slavery. Keep in mind, slavery ended in the U.S. more than 130 years ago. There isn't a living black person (born in the U.S.) who was ever a slave. There isn't a living white person (born in the U.S.) who ever owned a slave.

These facts haven't stopped the hoaxsters from pushing their newest "Big Lie."

Using their Marxist, "Animal Farm" thinking caps, they argue that all blacks suffered as a result of slavery; that blacks—even those who never experienced it—were permanently damaged by the institution of slavery, and that there is no statute of limitations on such a crime against (black) humanity.

Putting aside all other considerations for the sake of brevity and accepting such premises, let us reason together.

While Jewish people alive today did not directly endure slavery, their ancestors did. They were enslaved to build the Pyramids of Egypt and such. Since the legalistic hoaxsters argue against statutes of limitations for claims going back more than one century past, why not go back fifty centuries and have all Jewish people make claim for reparations against all Egyptians?

And, not to disrespect revisionist black "historians" who claim the great Pyramids and other Egyptian discoveries and creations were made by black Africans (not by Semitic Egyptians), we can ask for reparations from the NAACP and other black supremacist organizations.

Memo to the ACLU: How about it?

DISINFORMATION, NONINFORMATION: MEDIA PROPAGANDA

Decades ago, we could count on the mainstream media to point out these idiotic situations. Today? Not a chance. When the media aren't pumping out information to aid the al-Qaida terrorist network, or preoccupied with a priest scandal, they are peddling disinfo or the newest technique of the left-wing controlled press, "noninformation."

Case in point. A Filipino immigrant went berserk in the San Francisco Bay Area. He took out his handgun and shot two of his neighbors. The motive? The media blamed his depressed state of mind.

He was plagued by depression, they say.

His drugs weren't having the right effect.

But, because he was a "person of color" they didn't emphasize the gun or his race, as they would have if the shooter had blue eyes and blond hair. This poor fellow's emotions were supposedly outside his control.

Instead of calling this a "hate crime," the media spun it as an involuntary act by someone who wasn't receiving proper drug therapy. At least they didn't blame the murders on his doctor for not prescribing the right antidepressant. Still, their meaning was clear: This man was the *victim* of neglect by a discriminatory establishment unconcerned with the needs of "minorities."

Another case in point about media manipulation: At the stroke of midnight on a Saturday night, California Governor "Red" Davis passed a heroin-needle exchange bill, bowing to pressure from the radical homosexual lobby. When Monday morning rolled around, you'd never know what really took place. The newspapers reported that Davis passed a touchy-feely nurses bill, completely ignoring the needle exchange.

Davis ran on a platform of centrism, claiming that he would not approve needle-exchange legislation because it would send the wrong message to our children. Apparently, the media feel we have no right to know about the governor's hypocrisy.

I must point out one more example of the "new media propaganda." This is how the left-wing, pro-disarming-you, antimilitary *New York Times* wrote the headline: "Police Say Man Interrupted While Trying to Choke Girl." That's the headline. Read it again. This time see if you can identify the nuance: "Police Say Man Interrupted While Trying to Choke Girl."

The man happened to be an off-duty police sergeant who saved the girl. But the *New York Times* wouldn't say "Police Interrupted Man Trying to Choke Girl." The *New York Times* wouldn't say "Police Hero Saves Girl from Maniac Trying to Choke Her."

When I grew up, the headline in the *Daily News* or the *Post* or the *Mirror* or the *Journal American* would have proudly said: "Hero Cop Saves Girl from Strangler."

Today they take these uplifting stories of hero cops and bury them in the back of the newspaper. Who makes the cover of the liberal newspapers of America? The perverts. The murderers. The welfare cheats. The louses. The sickos. The anti-American socialists. Anyone who burns the flag and pees on the grave of your grandfather.

That's who goes to the head of the class.

This propaganda is a primary reason why our children rarely catch a glimpse of true heroes and heroines. Only when something on the scale of 9/11 happens do the press begrudgingly give these brave souls a nod. That is why the media bias must be exposed and ridiculed.

As you'll see in the next chapter, I am deeply concerned about this government-media complex. Americans deserve a fair and free press. Especially when substantive issues such as racially identifying terrorists, the stem-cell debate, illegal immigration, and the human-cloning controversy are being discussed.

WHAT IS THE PERFECT CLONE?

We are entering a brave new world. You see, liberal, tolerant societies live in a sort of amoral, limitless universe. They don't understand that limits must be imposed upon them. You can go all the way back to the sexual freedom movement. Look what the sexual freedom movement has led to.

Can anyone argue that unlimited freedom is not, in itself, anarchy and suicidal when it comes to sexuality? Nobody can argue that. Not with the AIDS epidemic. I don't care which way you twist it. Unlimited sexual license has led to death. And unlimited cloning will lead to death.

Children have the right to be procreated, not produced.

They are not machines on an assembly line.

Embryo cloning is immoral, and it should be made illegal.

Those who forge ahead with this kind of experimentation should be jailed. It must be stopped at all costs. This is worse than bio-terrorism. Human cloning has more potential for disaster than bio-terrorism, as I'll demonstrate. Once again, the utopian visions that are being produced by the scientists do not include the potential for an experiment going awry as if it were a Frankenstein being produced.

What will happen when they produce infants who do not match up with some desired ideal of the perfect child? What *is* a "perfect" human? In my view, this is an extension of Hitler's dream. Don't think for one minute that this is not going to lead to euthanasia. Don't think for one minute that this is not going to produce a disaster for humanity—because it will.

Who do you think they're going to clone? A crippled child?

Oh no. They're going to clone a "perfect" child or a "perfect" man.

So who gets to decide what a perfect child looks like? Oh, let's just ask the scientists. They'll tell us. One might say it's the Aryan ideal. Another might say it's the African ideal. Another might say it's the Asian ideal. Another might say the gay is the perfect ideal.

So, what does the perfect clone look like?

And how many millions of reproductions do you want of the perfect clone? We the sheeple don't know the answers to these questions. But the psychopaths, who meddle with creativity on a level that should not be meddled with, think they are the gatekeepers of all knowledge.

They aren't.

We are approaching a point of no return here. What happens if they create dozens of deformed human specimens? What are we going to do with them? Care for them like the crack babies of the 1980s? Or, are we going to exterminate them?

Really?

Then some not-so-bright social engineer will ask, "Oh, you're gonna exterminate deformed human specimens? Why stop with deformed human specimens that are merely cloned? Why not exterminate naturally born human specimens that are deformed in the womb?"

Do you understand where we're going with this?

Social insanity and the death of a culture are where the liberal mind ultimately takes a nation who fails to resist. Radical social liberals want unlimited freedom for all pursuits, all endeavors, and all impulses. If we follow down those roads, we are guaranteed to wake up in the middle of a nightmare.

BRAINWASHED

Back in college, I remember Sartre and Camus were big in those days. You know, the existentialists. I had no idea that Sartre was a commie. He smoked French cigarettes, wore a worsted suit and looked sophisticated, like Jean Paul Belmando could have played him. They always talked with cigarettes and they had nice babes and then they wrote this leftist drivel that the intellectuals told you was great.

I did not know until twenty years later that he was a Communist. I was programmed with that garbage. Took me a lifetime to figure out I was brainwashed in school, and then it takes an even longer time to get un-brainwashed, to start seeing the world as it is. For example, unlike what all the potheads said, life on earth is not infinite. All of the mescaline brains misquoted Blake, who said, "If you cleanse the doors of perception, you will see life as it is: infinite."

It's not infinite. You die.

None of you want to die.

Everyone reading this book is afraid of a heart attack in his forties. Most everyone touches his chest at least once a day. *"Ooh, what was that? No! I don't want to leave the kids."* I'm serious. Once a day, every guy over forty in America touches his chest and asks, "Oh, what was that? Is that it? Am I—ooh, no, no!" He breaks out in a cold sweat in the car and grips the steering wheel until his hands are white.

Most people in their forties suffer from cardioneurosis. You know, endless exercise, vitamins this, anticholesterol, don't run too much—look at the watch, don't have too much sex, don't have too little sex, don't eat salami, don't have an egg.

Of course life on earth is not infinite. Everyone knows that.

You die and it's over. Okay, some say there's reincarnation. But you don't know it. That's the whole point. I finally figured it out. For years, I was a do-gooder with religion in my own head. "Oh, yeah, I'm gonna lead a regular, good, saintly life because so-and-so says there's reincarnation, and I don't want to come back as Charlie Schumer. Or, God forbid, Barbara Boxer. If God punished me, he wouldn't give me a penis, and I'd have to be a female senator selling abortion clinics."

It's a terrible thing to contemplate that we come back as an il-liberal New York senator who goes west and pulls the wool over people's eyes. Or, say, as a crippled Taliban with one arm who is forced to fight alongside the other guys who have two. Or maybe as a bug like a centipede. I'm positive that Democrats come back as arthropods. And depending on how bad a Democrat they are, they go down the chain of arthropodism.

Anyway, as I said, none of you want to die.

I don't blame you. You and I are living in extraordinary times. Liberalism aside, there's so much to live for in this blessed land. Yes, these are truly historic times. Let me be specific. Look at the amazing events—good and bad—I have lived through, or inventions that I've seen, over the course of my lifetime (listed in no particular order):

1. "Superman" defeated by "everyman" in World War II

2. First atomic bomb used in warfare

3. The establishment of the State of Israel

4. Popularization of television

5. Popularization of air-conditioning

6. Popularization of air travel

7. Popularization of the personal computer

8. The invention of the Internet

9. The assassinations of John F. Kennedy, Robert F. Kennedy, and Martin Luther King Jr.

10. The first man to walk on the moon

11. The mainstreaming of homosexuality

12. The complete integration of blacks and whites

13. The development of mass welfare for unproductive citizens

14. The destruction of America's judicial system by corrupt lawyers

15. The meltdown of America's border controls

16. The self-genocide of America's European American majority through mass abortion and mass tolerance of "diverse" sexualities

17. The acceptance of narcotics

18. The debasement of religion

19. The takeover of corporations by gamblers and con men

20. The elimination of grades in many schools

21. The introduction of racial quota systems

22. The impeachment of a president

There is no place on earth like America. We have so much to be grateful for, which means We the People have much to defend. Remember my story of the French "chef" who insisted on serving me sushi? In like fashion, there are those in our midst—the RDDBs, the libs, the czarinas—whose only purpose in life is to ram something down our throats that we don't want, namely, socialism. Or, simply, to upset the established social order.

I won't let them. Not on my watch. Why?

Let me answer it this way. I remember the night my dad brought home my first car. It was raining, but that didn't stop me from going out to sit in it. This beauty was a used 1957 Oldsmobile two-door. It was a businessman's car, which was a little depressing because I wanted the coupe with the hardtop. At least my dark green car had the fire-rocket engine. Sitting behind the wheel, I felt as if my car were some kind of monolith from Mars.

I can still picture the rain droplets forming on the window. I sat there until 2:30 in the morning thinking, *Look at my car. Look how great I look in my car.* I thought everyone going by on the road saw me in that car, even though it wasn't moving. From day one, I took pride in that car. I figured my father must have worked hard to get it for me, and I was grateful to him.

Right then and there, I had to make a decision. See, I knew I was given something valuable that someone else had worked for. With it, I could hot-rod my way through the streets of Queens, just like the hoodlums down the block. I could skip the oil changes, forget about the tire pressure, and use cheap gas.

Or, I could take pride in the gift. I could read the owner's manual and learn how to maintain it properly. I could wash and wax it. I could keep small kids on bicycles from scratching the fenders. That night, I knew I had a choice to make.

Would I preserve and protect what was passed on to me?

Or would I do my own thing and squander the gift?

When it comes to America's borders, language, and culture, that's the question every American must ask of himself or herself. I happen to be someone who takes pride in America—who will do everything in his power to protect it and pass it on with a clean bill of health.

9

CRIMES OF
THE DEMOCRATS

❧

My dad was a Democrat.

My mom was a Democrat.

Most of my relatives still vote Democrat.

To an immigrant family, whose parents came of age during the Great Depression, President Franklin Delano Roosevelt was the Great White Savior. Aside from being the only U.S. president reelected to office three times, he gained lasting political mileage with the relief that his "New Deal" offered.

As you might expect, then, my father used to tell me, "Michael, all I know is, the Democrats are for the little guy, and the Republicans are for big business." So, as a young man, I voted as my dad did since I didn't understand politics.

After college, I began my professional life as a social worker (I'll save that story for my next book). I was in for a real shock as I worked the streets. The widespread excesses of the welfare system, which I saw firsthand, served as the first signal that the generous welfare system was doing real damage to our country.

Later on, after writing many books and earning my Ph.D. at the University of California, I slammed into another ugly truth about liberalism. I discovered I could not gain a professorship even after applying many times. My crime?

I was a white male.

Affirmative action—a misguided liberal policy supposedly used to promote equal opportunity—almost destroyed my family and me. For here I was, a "man-child in the promised land," denied my birthright for matters of race. I maintain that affirmative action is an insult to the individual and cannot be supported on a moral or ethical level. This destructive policy will lead to the further weakening of America's greatness.

Keep in mind, I had a nearly perfect A average in my graduate courses. My dissertation was published in a major scientific journal. This combination would have automatically ushered me into the halls of academe in any other past generation. Unfortunately, the Democrats had put up signposts across America's universities that declared: *White males need not apply*.

When I looked into which party was pushing affirmative action, that is, granting scholarships and jobs to less-qualified women, minorities, and immigrants because of their sex and gender, *I found the balance sheet completely skewed in favor of the Republicans*.

Until quite recently, the Republicans favored quality and qualifications over socialism, while the Democrats preferred a "color-coded America" over a "quality-coded America."

Today the lines have become quite blurred. Both parties raised tens of millions of dollars from big business while trying to appeal to the "little guy." Both parties try to identify themselves as representing "the workingperson." And yet, while we seem to have an operational oligarchy party, "Republicats" and "Demicans" (your choice), there are subtle differences worth noting.

In my book, the Republicans win because they're less likely to seize our guns, less likely to raise our taxes, less likely to support infanticide (so-called late-term abortion); they offer less regulation by big government, are more likely to support traditional family values and, as recent history has demonstrated, more likely to actually mail a tax-refund check to you.

Unfortunately, on the issue of granting amnesty to illegal immigrants, both parties are pandering to the illegal-alien lobby. However, the subtle differences I mentioned above make it worth strongly considering the Republicans over the Democrats.

Why do these small differences make all the difference?

As a man who loves boating, I understand how only a few degrees in a course change result in huge implications down the way. You see, while the change in course is very slight when you first, say, turn a few degrees to the right, as you follow the new course the arc of change gradually becomes larger and larger. What appeared to be only a few degrees of change at the point of origin become an enormous arc of difference later on.

That is why the few degrees that separate the Democrats and the Republicans are so important. And so, as a registered Independent, I have to go with the party that grants me more liberty. The evidence is in. The Democratic Party, driven by liberalism, is an express train to tyranny.

HIJACKING THE ELECTION

Although I am a bipartisan basher and have been highly critical of the Republicans' liberal leanings, I have to go with the Republicans over the Democrats for the reasons I express in this chapter. Take the last national election. I remember being in West Palm Beach, Florida, on November 10, 2000, to be with my mom. It was right in the middle of the South Florida ballot controversy. The timing couldn't have been better.

In memorializing this Florida vote battle, I wrote the following for my radio show. I call it "Can of Worms."

> Thirty-eight states said "Yes" to Bush.
> Twelve states said "Yes" to Gore.
> Are some states more equal than other states?

South Florida.

Where millionaires grifting off the welfare state pretend to each other
the moral indignation of the downtrodden
Lexus liberals with Volkswagens on the brain.
Condo Commies, Lunchroom Lenins, Stand-Up Stalins,
Miserable Maos.
Stealing ballots, grifting SSI, faking disabilities,
voting for Al Gore—all in a day's work.
South Florida.
The Land of Sunshine, Schmoozing, and now Stupidity.
The whole world now knows New York Democrats are too stupid to
vote straight but smart enough to twist the truth when
their "benefits" are threatened.
South Florida.
The Land of Suntanned Trotskys in Delis.
Bypassed Bolsheviks in Buicks. Air-Conditioned Chés in Condos. Loud,
lewd losers in limbo. Stuck between their investments and their liberal-
ism. Lost to God, fervent in their nonbelief
except in the DNC, their new religion.
South Florida.
Corned-Beef Commies, Buffet Bolshies,
Jogging Jokesters, stuck in Camelot fantasies.
Kennedy, their last idol, a drunk, profligate warmonger
covered for by his classy wife.
Hillary, their Evita Peron.
Bill, their shameless shaygitz.
Tipper their tipsy doughnut. Al their shabbos goy.
South Florida.
The Land of Sun and SOBs.
Crooked Chiropractors, Degenerate Dentists
Medicare Medicos, Harlot Heart Surgeons
Nutty Neurologists, Craven Cardiologists
Improbable Proctologists, Petty Pornographers

Huge Urologists, Incensed Internists
Demoncats, all!
Strip clubs in strip malls,
Lantana hedges hiding black-glassed assets.
South Florida.
The Land of Sun and stolen votes.

Need I remind you that the Dems attempted to steal the election in 2000? Who could forget how they made a huge issue about lost and stolen ballot boxes. I remember speaking to the Savage Nation about this fabricated left-wing controversy. Let's learn from history because, as we've been told, those who don't know their history are condemned to repeat it.

You've got to understand how incredibly fortunate your Savage was to be in Florida and, amazingly, in Palm Beach County where the future of the nation hung in the balance by a loose chad. While I was there, I remember getting reports from across Palm County of undercounted votes. We learned that Jesse Hijackson found a lost ballot box. It was stuffed, no doubt, with votes of dead crack dealers.

We heard from Congressman Wexler, another sterling Democrat. This one from Florida via Brooklyn and NYU Law. We learned Congressman Wexler had apparently found a sunken Spanish galleon off the Florida coast. On it, miraculously, was another ballot box, waterproof, of course, stuffed with the votes of deceased Spanish sailors.

The sailors were all Gore men. Centuries ago, you see, with the aid of a psychic these sailors envisioned a Señor Gore who would come to save the New Lands. According to the congressman, all the deceased Spanish sailors converted from Christianity to a New World religion called Democraticism!

They became proto-Democrats over four hundred years ago.

And lo, they voted for Al Gore. Of course, that meant their

votes would be tallied along with the living dead Democrats of today's Florida. Where prescription drugs for free will set you free—North Korea's nukes not withstanding.

I also remember I was the only one to expose the *real* story: The Dems claimed that the ballot machines themselves were racist, sexist, and homophobic!

Racist, because some blacks could say the ballots did not self-punch "Gore" when sensing extra melanin on their hands. Racist, because some elderly Jewish voters may have thought "Gore" meant "Gornisht" so they did not pick that presidential candidate.

The ballot machines were homophobic because some weak-wristed types had insufficient strength to press hard enough to register a vote—commonly referred to as a "pregnant chad."

And, as we later learned, the ballot machines were sexist because they were too, well, technical, favoring linear or "masculine" thought processes, thereby confusing some women.

DEMS PROMOTE VOTER FRAUD

Voter fraud isn't limited to Florida—nor is it a joke. It's running rampant in America, and it's destroying the backbone of our electoral process. Recently, I went into my local polling booth and gave one of the volunteers my name. As I looked around, the "voter officials" were old ladies—all liberals, of course—from the League of Women Voters. Their job is to make sure Republican ballots are treated unfairly.

You think I'm kidding?

I overheard one woman say to her assistant, "How is he registered?" She whispered back, "Independent." The first hag looked at me with glaring alarm, as if an alien had walked into the voting booth. Not because they knew who I was, but because I was not a registered Democrat!

Here in Taliban County, not far from Rat Boy's high school, if anyone says he is not a Democrat, I'm surprised that they don't call the police, release attack dogs, and turn on the fire hoses!

Anyway, I pulled out my driver's license and asked her, "Would you like to see my ID?"

The old gray lady with tennis sneakers said, "Oh, no."

I said, "What do you mean, 'Oh, no'? How do you know I am who I say I am? I am trying to defend the voting system."

"Oh, no," she said. "We don't need to see that."

In America we have lost that which your ancestors died for—our sacred right to vote. If you offer your photo ID and have it refused, you might be considered to be committing a hate crime. Here's the illogic.

In the upside-down, Alice-in-Wonderland world, ruled by psychotic liberals, *voter fraud* is considered a *civil right*. If you try to prevent voter fraud, it is considered a hate crime. The liberals have destroyed our voting system, and I can prove it. In the interest of full disclosure, I am going to name names.

A Republican bill introduced into the Senate would have required a photo ID for anyone who wants to vote. We know that photo IDs can be faked, but we know that it is much better than just a signature. Still, there are at least two public enemies with regard to reforming election fraud. Take a guess which two U.S. senators are trying to block the use of photo IDs for voters.

None other than "Upchuck" Schumer in New York, the ambulance chaser, the man with no shame, the man who looks like he just got out of a courtroom after settling a chain accident for illegal immigrants. On the West Coast, it's Ron Wyden of Oregon who wants to block fixing the voting system.

You have to ask yourself, *Why?* Why would Wyden widen cheating on votes? Why would a radical liberal like Ron Wyden—who has ties to Enron auditor Arthur Andersen, want to preserve voter fraud? What's in it for the radical liberals?

The answer is simple.

Wyden said, "The 2000 ballot recount in Florida taught us that the goal of election reform should be to simplify the system and make it more inclusive. The narrow photo ID requirement of the election reform bill could effectively straitjacket voters, not just in Oregon, but across the country. That's why I have offered the amendment to allow more flexibility."

The key word here is *inclusive,* which is a code word for "illegal alien and those not entitled to vote." The phrase "narrow photo ID requirement" is another giveaway that he is trying to permit illegal aliens to vote.

Ron Wyden and Upchuck Schumer should be censured by the United States Senate for blocking voter reform.

For many years we have screamed, "Stop the illegal votes! Stop the illegals from voting! Stop the vote scam!" Now we know who is protecting the vote scammers: Ron Wyden and Upchuck Schumer. How you liberals, who claim to love liberty, can vote for these two, I don't know.

Wyden wants the system to be more "inclusive"? Does that include the Arabs who come here to kill us?

Is that what he wants? Does he want to give those who want to bomb us the right to vote with fake IDs? What kind of inclusion do you mean, Mr. Wyden?

I want you to read another thing that Wyden has to say: "The goal of this Amendment is to make certain that overly stringent identification requirements . . ."

Wait a minute. How can you have "overly stringent" identification requirements? Nobody's asking for a urine sample. We're talking a photo ID—the same thing you provide a pharmacist when you write a check to buy your Prozac.

Ron Wyden says, "The goal of this Amendment is to make certain that overly stringent identification requirements do not disenfranchise eligible voters or compromise Oregon's and Washington's unique mail ballot systems." Care to take a guess which national organizations oppose the photo ID requirements?

- The League of Women Voters in the U.S., a radical front group
- The Leadership Conference on Civil Rights, a radical front group
- The American Association of Retired Persons, a radical pressure group
- The National Hispanic Leadership Agenda, a radical socialist group
- The National Council of La Raza, a racist group
- The Mexican-American Legal Defense and Education Fund, an anti-American racist group
- The NAACP Legal Defense Fund, an anti-white pressure group

In my opinion, each of the above groups favors maintaining voter fraud. They do not want your vote to remain sacred. They want to make certain that those *not eligible* to vote can continue to skew elections and put in power rats and skunks of the type we have now.

The Republicans, answering the call of the American citizen, have tried to put in a sensible photo ID requirement. The radical left-wing harpies are trying to block even this. They are traitors and should be investigated by the Senate. I only wish we had a Senator McCarthy to uncover their true loyalty.

How did we get in this mess?

The voting system started hundreds of years ago. Back then, the election judges and poll watchers in a given town knew most everyone in their precincts and could vouch for their identity. In modern America, this community intimacy is virtually nonexistent. It's insane that identification for voting in America today is still based on the honor system. That's why our election process is totally bankrupt and voter fraud is out of control.

In a time of widespread corruption, in a time of war, in a time where we are riddled with ten to fifteen million illegal aliens, these left-wing radicals still say we need the honor system. Adding insult to injury, signatures, if taken, are not compared to a signature on file in most places, unless you are challenged by election judges or poll watchers, which rarely happens. Then again, your signature *and* a DNA sample may be required if you are a white male and a registered republican.

What are you going to do when you wake up one day and find out your country has been stolen from you?

IMAGINE AL GORE IN CHARGE

During the election cycle of 2000, the Demoncats' legal shenanigans wasted millions of taxpayer dollars on counting, recounting, and recounting a third time the punch cards, not to mention the financial burden on the judicial system.

Let's pretend that this costly debacle gave them the White House. Could you imagine if Al Gore and Tipper were in charge of America today? Could you imagine what trouble we'd be in? Can you guess how we'd be doing in a "Big Al vs. al-Qaida" matchup?

I can't. Al Gore just seems to find, and then listen to, the worst advice. Take his image consulting. It was bad enough during the campaign where he reinvented himself fifty times. But after he lost, the guy comes back out of obscurity looking like Paul Bunyan. Who told him to grow a beard? We'll never know. We can only assume it was his daughter. Maybe Dick Morris, or maybe it was some other wacko toe-sucking consultant who came up with it.

I can just imagine the advice:

"You know, Al, the whole presidency thing, we need a strong father figure so I would think that you should grow a beard because you're big and you're macho. Look, you kinda have that Abe Lincoln vibe, if only you had a beard. Maybe you could get really pumped on steroids, too . . ."

So, the guy comes back with a beard.

"Hello, I'm Al Gore."

You know, the whole thing was over the edge. Could you picture this guy if he were president now? Sweating up there, having to take six showers? Six showers a day, changing the towels in every hotel he ever went to?

Okay, we all know it's not about Al Goreleone, head of the Goreleone Crime Syndicate. Gore, we must remember, is "his own man." No, our concern is about his *agenda*. In fact, I recently imagined a highly classified document from Al's personal journal which spelled out what America might anticipate with Al Gore in the White House.

GORE'S CONTRACT AGAINST AMERICA

1. Homosexuals in the military and homosexual marriage

2. Affirmative action, or *The Fairness for Dummies Act*

3. Reparations for non-slaves by non-slaveholders

4. Hate-crime laws aimed at straight, white males

5. Racial profiling laws, aimed at straight, white police

6. A United Nation's tax or a world tax

7. Free prescription drugs not only for the elderly but also for AIDS patients

8. Delegitimizing the Boy Scouts, or *The Fairness to Predators Act*

9. Outlawing homeschooling, or *The Freedom from Learning Act*

10. Arrest, ban, or rewrite the authentic Bible as a hate book

11. Mandatory application of Ritalin to any child with spunk, or *The Security for Children Act*

12. Complete elimination of borders with Mexico, or *The Fairness to Latinos Act*

13. Partial-birth abortion or infanticide and the sale of baby body parts, or *The Senior Citizen Life Extension Act*

14. Increased license for Hollywood's violence and pornography, or *The Freedom of Arts Act*

15. Socialized medicine and a national health plan, or *The Freedom from Bad Behavior Act*

16. *The No Limits on Lawsuits Act*

17. Mandatory suicide for sick seniors, or *The Saving Social Security Act*

18. *The Fairness in Talk Radio Act*, i.e., the end of talk radio

19. The end of the Electoral College and the congressional redistricting of America to ensure that never again will the Demoncats be threatened, or *The One Dunce, One Vote Act*

20. The complete seizing of all guns, or *The Freedom from the Second Amendment Act*

21. The abolition of our existing Constitution or *The Freedom from Freedom Act*

GORE'S DEGENERATE SOCIETY

Can the U.S. ever recover from the damage done to it by the Democrats? It has taken us thirty years to begin recovering from the damage done by LBJ and the Warren Court liberals. "The Great Society" of LBJ, which was Mao-Lite, led us to "the Degenerate Society" of the Gores.

Red Diaper Doper Baby lawyers seized power. Criminals were given more freedoms than cops. Junk lawsuits proliferated. Too many schoolchildren lost the ability to add, spell, or write.

Pornography penetrated every home with a TV or computer. Violence became the national sport. Athletes, once role models, became models of ghetto trash. Sex, once sacred, became a cheap sneeze in the night. Unborn babies were slaughtered, their body parts sold for profit by factories of death. Diseased and criminal immigrants flooded into America. White males were scapegoated as the incarnation of evil. Voting was rigged, and turnout fell to new lows. Free speech disappeared. Thought crimes were targeted. Monopolies appeared in all major industries.

America's moral standing was destroyed. War crimes against the Serbs were committed in Yugoslavia. The U.S. media, once a watchdog, became a tool of the Democrats. The jewels of our nuclear secrets were sold to China for donations to the Gore campaign and the Democratic National Committee.

Now, as I said, it has taken us thirty years to *begin* correcting just some of the social damage done by LBJ's army of do-gooders who did very bad, indeed.

How long might it take us to correct the damage done by the Gore Democrats? Will we ever know how deeply they have injured the nation? Not until and unless the Democrats' grip on the major media is broken by antitrust legislation.

The Degenerate Society we have inherited from eight years of trickle-down immorality can be directly traced to Gore's straightman act, which enabled his boss to get away with all the shocks and outrages mentioned above. Not since the Weimar Republic of pre-Nazi Germany has decadence so completely permeated a free society.

I also predict, should Al, Hillary, or one of the other clueless con-men Demoncats win the presidency, Americans can expect the following:

- A steep rise in taxes everywhere

- Many more illegal aliens in every town and city

- Foreign spies in our science laboratories

- Islam-O-Fascism as protected speech

- Vouchers for government-mandated Diversity Training

There will also be a seizure of our constitutional right to protect our homes with guns. More race-based hiring, race-based scholarships, and race-based school admissions. Government-supplied Ritalin for boys who show signs of the disease called masculinity. The further rejection of God. More hate-crime legislation. More pornography in your living room.

And we mustn't forget more legal and illegal drugs. Or the de facto end to our national borders (except for customs taxation). Or churches and temples without worshipers (as in ancient Hellenistic Greece). Or less self-reliance and more reliance on "Big Sister."

In short: *The end of freedom . . . the next step to serfdom.*

All lubricated by the Democrat Party's contribution toward socialism.

COMMUNICATION

Do you know what the primary problem in life is between people, between nations, between parties, or between races? I tell you the most complex situations can be reduced to one word: *miscommunication.*

Now you may think, *Savage, you're getting soft and liberal.* No,

I'm serious. Of course, I know there are animals you can't communicate with. I know they'd eat your heart out no matter what you did or said to them. In fact, I can tell you which groups on earth would cut your heart out and cook it in front of your wife.

They're called the Taliban. And that's why America, under George Bush, had to go and crush them.

We know that there are evil people on earth.

But, if you were to boil down most problems with, for instance, your relatives, I'd estimate 90 percent of your problems have to do with a matter of miscommunication. In the old days, Mom lived with the family as she got older. You and she lived in the same house—not halfway across the country in an "extended-care community."

Sure, you got on each other's nerves, but you understood each other. You heard a human being breathing in the other room, through the wall. You saw your mom struggling to walk. You saw how hard it was for her to get a drink of water. You also caught her smile, her tears of joy, her efforts to still show you love even after all these years.

How could you get mad (and stay mad) at your mother? Never. Unless you were insane.

Today, when you and she live thousands of miles apart, it's easy to start to take her disconnected statements, take her silences, take her tone and turn them into chasms that don't exist. Before you know it, you start to make them bigger than they are.

That's how, in simple terms, miscommunication happens.

Look at the differences between liberals and conservatives. Many of these differences are fundamental and can never be bridged. The chasm cannot be crossed in certain areas, I'll admit that. No amount of conversation will move me to the liberal viewpoint when it comes to pro-life, pro-traditional-family, or pro-Judeo-Christian values.

On the other hand, there *are* areas that we, with the help of improved communication, can agree on. There must be a way to find common ground on the matters of our borders, language, and culture. Fiscal responsibility, national security, race relations. Great strides can be made in each of these areas with better communication between liberals and conservatives. That's one reason I have the fastest-growing radio talk show in the nation. I'm encouraging the national dialogue on these key issues.

However, an example where I will likely "agree to disagree" with the liberals relates to Al Gore, his personal scandals, his junk science, his false claims (i.e., inventing the Internet, that *Love Story* was based on his romance with wife Tipper), and, as I'll discuss next, his violations of ethics.

GORE'S OCCIDENTAL OIL SCANDAL

One doesn't have to look far to find a prime example of Gore's incompetence as a leader and his questionable ethics. For example, as vice president, Al Gore endorsed the sale of a government oil field in 1998, the largest sale of federal property in the history of the U.S. government.

The Elk Hills Naval Petroleum Reserve, located near Bakersfield, California, was established in 1912 to help fuel navy ships. The president proposed the sale in 1995, saying the oil field no longer served a military purpose.

The U.S. Department of Energy (DOE) received a total of twenty-two bona fide offers but decided to sell this "crown jewel" of oil and gas fields to Occidental Petroleum Corp. By selling off this resource the Gore team eliminated the U.S. Navy's primary source of emergency crude oil. They argued that this field "no longer serves a national security purpose."

"We view this asset as becoming the crown jewel of our domestic operations," said Occidental Oil and Gas CEO David Hentschel.

Couching this questionable attack on our National Security in conservative jargon, DOE's Assistant Secretary for Fossil Energy Patricia Godley claimed the sale was part of Al Gore's efforts to "reduce the size of government" and "return inherently non-federal functions to the private sector." The largest-ever federal divestiture was also said to help "pay off the national debt."

The sale of this government oil field to Occidental Petroleum may have directly benefited Al Gore through his ownership of Occidental stock. While his aides denied Gore encouraged this sale, his *Reinventing Government* called on the government to sell these precious oil reserves. "Elk Hills Naval Petroleum Reserves . . . no longer serves its original strategic purpose for the navy," wrote Gore.

Gore called for the sale of this prime contingency source of fuel for the navy, calling it "commonsense government." In an emergency, where will our navy get its fuel? From Iraq?

The same Al Gore witnessed the loss, theft, or sale of the crown jewels of our nuclear war know-how from Los Alamos National Laboratory. Whether these events are interconnected we do not know. That our national security has been seriously damaged is a certainty.

Again, this should not come as a surprise.

Whether misestimating the capacity and value of our national oil supply, or exaggerating the extent of damage to the ozone layer around the earth, Al Gore gets an A+ in junk science. The guy is nuts. When it comes to physical science, everything he learned at Harvard must have been bogus.

For years, Al staked out his claim as the protector of the environment. He wrote extensively about the need to rescue earth from global warming and the depletion of the ozone. He claimed these issues were "the central organizing principle for civilization." Really?

More important than terrorism?

World hunger?

The breakdown of the family?

In Gore's mind, evidently, yes. He called for an "all-out effort to use every policy and program, every law and institution, every treaty and alliance" to combat the evils of global warming and the ozone depletion.

Even when faced with the facts to the contrary, Gore stated, "The evidence of global warming keeps piling up, month after month, week after week."

Al says the sky is falling.

The press dutifully report the news.

Al says there's a giant hole in the ozone layer.

The press take it as gospel.

Al says we're all gonna die because of the ozone hole . . .

Not so fast. A handful of scientists started to dig around for the truth. Guess what they found: Al's head is lost somewhere on Cloud Nine. The guy's a complete dreamer.

According to scientists from Tokyo University, the ozone hole should mend completely by the year 2040. They used a super-computer to assess and model projected atmospheric conditions around the globe. Their research predicts that the hole in the ozone layer will remain constant for fifteen years before modest changes will occur, ultimately paving the way to a full regeneration.

No more hole—except in Al's theory.

Why won't Al, the global warming bogeyman, back down?

Because this presidential hopeful is in search of an issue he can champion. Gore would rather hold on to a theory that has long since been debunked, than admit the damage to ozone levels will be reversed.

One senator from Colorado, allied with Al's global warming crusade, gave this advice: "We've got to ride the global warming issue. Even if the global warming theory is wrong, we will be doing the right thing anyway in terms of economic policy and environmental policy."

Do you understand what these demagogues are saying?

Do you understand where they are going?

If enough of the sheeple can be convinced to accept Gore's Big Lie, Gore will have an easier time selling additional government controls to "defend and preserve" the ozone. A compliant sheeple will give him the "mandate" to drag our country into the disastrous Kyoto Accord, which, in turn, allows Gore to slap us with regulations to minimize future damage to the ozone.

Maybe he'd outlaw all autos larger than a Yugo.

Maybe he'd raise taxes on gas to discourage automobile usage.

Maybe he'd tax anybody who didn't ride a bike to work.

Maybe he'd ban the use of air conditioners and pass out hand fans.

Maybe he'd issue government-regulated thermostats for your home.

It's all about growing the size of government. It's all about turning the clock backward and making America a Third World nation. Then, and only then, will we be "doing the right thing."

GORE'S TEN CRIMES

During one of his past presidential debates, Al Gore was asked to identify what he considered the most memorable moments of the century. He muttered something unintelligible about "Vietnam" and "Social Security."

This would-be president didn't mention Edison's invention of the lightbulb, Ford's assembly line, the Wright Brothers' first flight, the atom bomb, or the development of the telephone, radio, television, or computer! Neither did he mention the defeat of Hitler or the destruction of the Soviet Evil Empire (by Ronald Reagan). To Al Gore, this sideshow freak in the great circus called liberalism, only social programs that take from one group and give to another are considered "great events of the century."

We should not be shocked, then, that under eight years of Gore, the following inexcusable events took place. I call them Gore's Ten Crimes:

1. Chinese military operatives stole, bought, or were openly given the jewels of our nuclear secrets.

2. Illegal immigrants from the Middle East, Mexico, China, Africa, and Central America broke through our borders.

3. Homosexual radicals were allowed to attack America's children—e.g., the Boy Scouts.

4. Leftist radicals were permitted to falsely accuse our police.

5. Islam-O-Fascists entered our country through a defacto open border policy.

6. The ACLU was permitted to steal the votes of six million Californians who voted to eliminate free medication and free education for illegal immigrants.

7. The ACLU was encouraged to drive Christianity out of churches, prayer off playing fields, babies out of wombs, and pornography into every home.

8. Babies near birth were slaughtered, their body parts sold for profit.

9. Innocent Serbian children were bombed and killed.

10. The Fourth Amendment was thrown out so little Elian Gonzalez's door could be kicked in without due process.

Crimes 11 through 100 to be continued . . .

CRIMES OF THE DEMOCRATS

ELIAN:
THE ONLY IMMIGRANT THE DEMOCRATS HATED

Every chance the Demoncats get, they make sure the sheeple know how "compassionate" they are. With bleeding hearts, the Dems stand before the cameras to announce how much they care about "the little guy."

How is it, then, that the Clinton-Gore administration, which had been more lenient toward millions of immigrants than any in the history of this nation, had such a vendetta against little Elian Gonzalez?

A review of the facts is instructive. It's interesting that there were several survivors who had clung to the raft before it was rescued. Did you know that all of the other survivors were granted asylum in America; yet this little boy was given the bum's rush by the Demoncats. Obviously the boy was a trophy for Fidel Castro.

Anyone who has studied the issue knows full well that the Democrats sent Elian back to a Marxist prison called Cuba in order to avoid another Marielle boat exodus. Why did so many of the American sheeple side with the Clinton-Gore team on this issue?

The answer can be found in the term "psycho politics."

It is a term that was coined in a speech before American students at Lenin University in Moscow a half century ago by Lavrenty Pavlovich Beria, Deputy Premiere of the Soviet Union and head of the NKVD (secret police) under Joseph Stalin.

Psycho politics has been used in America in the following manner. As Beria taught, "You must labor until you have dominion over the minds and bodies of every important person in your nation." Using the power of the media, which increasingly parrots the voice of the Democrats, psycho politics has come to rule in America.

The United States Constitution—especially the Fourth Amendment—was clearly violated in the illegal INS Border Patrol machine-gun raid in the Gonzalez home in Miami. Yet most Americans, owing to the constant stream of propaganda, or psycho politics, from the government media complex, have come to view this kid-napping as a rescue.

We Americans live in an extremely dangerous time, when the radical Democrat cronies steal a page from Lavrenty Beria's notes.

DASHING DASCHLEGATE

The crimes of the Democrats continue to pile up.

Take Dashing Tom Daschle, the Senate Majority Leader.

Tommy Daschle, who plays the part of Mr. Moderate, Mr. Centrist, hopes you won't connect the dots between his lobbyist wife, Linda, and the companies she represents, including airlines, aircraft makers, and other aviation-related interests.

Funny how these liberal pirates work the system.

Each of the industries Linda represents *also* has a steady stream of issues before Congress for consideration, and guess who holds the power to set the Senate's agenda? Old Dashing Daschle.

Linda Daschle says she will deal with that potential pitfall by never lobbying her husband or any member or committee of the Senate. She says she feels very "comfortable" with her activities.

Really, now. She probably feels about as comfortable as Dianne Feinstein does with her husband, Richard Blum, who does mega business with China. Am I right, Linda? What makes Linda Daschle's case compelling is that her client list includes, among others, Loral Space and Technologies and Intelli-Check. Both are government contractors who circle the White House like hungry dogs waiting to be fed fat government contracts.

Linda's bedmate schedules the feedings in the Senate.

For the record, Loral Space and Technologies transferred much of our highly classified information to communist China, giving the communist Chinese the ability to aim with greater accuracy their intercontinental ballistic missiles—at us!

Is Dashing Daschle concerned about this?

Not in the least.

He was more concerned over the photograph of President Bush fielding calls from *Air Force One* during 9/11—a historical event—which the Republicans have sold (that's capitalism at its best), than he is of his wife's closed-door, strong-arm tactics that have added muscle thanks to the Senate Majority Leader.

To Dashing Daschle, the sale of the Bush photo is "a very serious ethical violation." As to his wife's conflicts of interest, this cheap suit with pancake makeup offers only a shrug of indifference.

The facts are unmistakable. Certain companies are throwing secret amounts of money to Linda Daschle to line her pocketbook, violating all tenets of decency. She's declined to disclose the identity of the companies or the amounts they've paid for her "services" as a lobbyist.

I have no problem with lobbyists who represent the company or cause of their choice. But the fact that the Daschles refuse to voluntarily disclose the sources of income smacks of scandal and a conflict of interest. In the face of public pressure, these people stall, play dodgeball, mince words and, in the end, refuse disclosure. Why the secrecy? Is there a quid pro quo?

Of course, this is just more of the Daschle "noninformation" technique, a favorite gimmick of today, as I've pointed out before, to distract us from the true nature of the left agenda. But regardless of one's agenda, I say such secret money has no place in American politics.

It's one more example of the blatant arrogance of Tom Daschle and his wife, who have no honor or shame. The American system will collapse—this is no exaggeration—if such shady, underhanded dealings are allowed to continue. I promise, these actions will destroy our fragile democracy. We must put a stop to the abuses of the Daschles and any others who thumb their nose at the American people and the rule of law and decency.

If you think it can't happen here, you're sadly mistaken.

Or, take the hysteria exhibited by Daschle in September 2002. He went on the Senate floor to decry a *mistaken* quote that President Bush never made! "We're not interested in National Security?" he screamed. "Tell that to Senator Inouye, tell that to those who served in Vietnam . . . I recently went to Normandy" to see the graves, etc. By the time he was finished you would think that Daschle had *personally* lost an arm in WWII, lost both legs in Vietnam, and that he was buried in Normandy!

MICROSOFT TO BE
MICRO-MANAGED BY MICRO MINDS?

I'm not for monopoly capitalism, by any means. But I do support equal protection under the law. I want to know why, under the Democratic leadership, some corporations are singled out for antitrust suits while other corporations—sometimes as large or larger—are totally ignored. Who makes these decisions?

Who, for example, decided to go after Bill Gates and Microsoft while letting other firms, as large or larger, even multinational conglomerates, sneak by unnoticed? Democratic weasels pretend they were helping consumers when they viciously attacked Microsoft, but they were acting out a vendetta.

Why didn't the Dems go after other industries in which monopoly capitalism might be at work? Look at the major media. We've seen recent media mergers, awesome in size and scope, that with the formation of a new media giant virtually eliminated the competition. It's a fact that media companies are among the greatest examples of monopoly in existence.

Fewer and fewer hands are controlling more and more outlets, crushing independent voices, squeezing the life out of freedoms of the press and speech. Why, then, is there no such attack by the Democrats and the U.S. Justice Department against the new media monopolies? Whether in our schools, in government, or over the airwaves, the media spew the same Socialist-lite messages nonstop. And we're to believe the government-media complex is not a monopoly!

Obviously, Gates didn't cultivate the right people. Even with his one-billion-dollar "gift" to the United Negro College Fund he didn't line the right pockets, on the left side of the aisle or the right. So they gave him the royal shakedown. (I don't own Microsoft stock—never have.)

Al Capone used to shake down saloon owners who refused to buy his booze: "Hey! Buy our beer, or we'll redecorate your establishment! What's it gonna be?"

There's really little difference in what's happened to Microsoft. Like Capone with the saloons, the liberal Democrat gang has got you no matter how you answer: The antitrust laws in America make it illegal to charge more than the competition. It's called price gouging. But you can't charge less, either, because that would be undercutting your competitors. And if you charge the same, then you're guilty of collusion. They've got you crated and ready for delivery no matter which way you turn.

The government, by its nature, is an anti-free enterprise. Our Founding Fathers knew this well. They considered the government an evil necessity. That's why they did everything they could to limit and counterbalance its powers by our Constitution. If left to its own devices, government is itself monopolistic and inevitably tries to stifle innovation. That's why it covers for its fellow monopolies, the true monopolies with which it is in collusion, while going after firms like Microsoft that might threaten the established power structure.

Until enough of us learn this simple truth, we'll continue down the slippery slope toward true monopolism, toward totalist government, where Microsoft will be the least of our worries. The left calls it fascism, the right calls it socialism. But once you've slid over the edge, it makes little difference whether you call it a pit or a hole.

The weasels on the left pretend they are helping consumers, but they are obviously acting out some sort of vendetta. Some critics have suggested Bill Gates did not donate much, if anything, to the Democratic National Committee.

America is fast developing a mandarin class that seeks to suffocate the greatness of people like Bill Gates and others who have made us a great nation. Let me explain.

In approximately A.D. 1000, China led the world both in a relatively free economy and in innovation. They had six-masted sailing ships. They were producing more coal in China in the year 1000 than Britain produced in the year 1600. This great advancement came to a grinding halt over the next one hundred or so years.

The decline of China's advancements can be laid to the mandarin class, which ruled China with iron fingernails.

The mandarins, as you may remember, were a small group of elites who ruled the entire nation in the same sort of centralized bureaucratic fashion we now see in America. They stifled innovation and overtaxed the innovators, so they snuffed out China's great advances for well over a thousand years.

If we are to maintain our advantages as the most advanced civilization, we must make it very clear that We the People will not tolerate the new mandarin class in America. We the People must regulate the regulators—whether they are Demicans or Republicrats.

LIEBERMAN'S CHOICE:
THE RED AND THE BLACK

For decades, the atheistic, anti-God, antifamily, anti-mom-and-pop feathers of the Democratic Party's left wing have told us about the dangers of permitting God to enter the political arena. They have created a climate of religious intolerance today unmatched in our nation's history.

Hating the "religious right" more than Islam-O-Fascism, these crazed antichurch fanatics swoop in to prevent Christian boys from conducting a quick prayer on the ball field. Next thing you know, they'll send out informants to see if you're praying in your own home over a meal.

Enter a Democrat Party hack who used his religion as a weapon. And when he did, we heard not a murmur about church and state from the media elite. Why? Because "Saint Lieberman" comes out of the "religious left." You see, the complaints by liberals were never about keeping *religion* out of politics. It was about keeping *conservative religious tenets* out of politics.

How many times did you hear the following: "Senator Lieberman is a very moral man. He's an orthodox Jew"?

Why don't we hear: "Reverend Falwell has been a moral force in America for decades. He is a devout Baptist"?

Political orientation is the key. Simply put, Lieberman is a left-wing party hack; Falwell is a conservative.

On abortion and the homosexual agenda, Lieberman is in direct conflict with orthodox Jewish law and tradition. He is a hypocrite who uses his religious affiliation to push left-wing views, even though his political orientation conflicts with his religious orientation.

In the novel *The Red and the Black* by the French writer Stendhal, the protagonist realizes that, in order to rise in French society on the eve of the July revolution of 1830, an ambitious young man has to make a choice: the red uniform of the military or the black frock of the church. He chooses the path of the church to make his social climb.

Lieberman seems to wear his orthodoxy on his sleeve in an attempt to bully his political opponents into submission.

For Lieberman, like the black-garbed character in the French novel, religion seems to be a means, not an end in itself.

THE NEW HUMANITY?

The pro-death Democrat Party plank on abortion (mislabeled pro-choice) has been lengthened by several outspoken liberal Demoncats who favor the inclusion of infanticide. Once we blast through that pro-life fire wall, insanity awaits the nation. How? If, God forbid, infanticide is accepted and practiced in America, the *right*-to-die movement will rejoice and quickly begin their efforts to advocate "the *duty*-to-die" movement.

Does that sound far-fetched?

It isn't.

Look at the facts.

The re-educators, brainwashers, and pioneers of the "New Humanity" are already filling key professorships in the liberal universities. And they spread their damnable hatred for life on the seminar circuit. Need proof?

Not long ago, a leader of the Democrat Party attended a seminar in Switzerland where Professor Peter Singer, distinguished scholar at "Youthanasia U." (Princeton), was among the honored speakers. Singer is distinguished not so much for studies in euthanasia—the "mercy" killing of the elderly—but for his advocacy of "youth-anasia," the killing of handicapped youth, in former times known as infanticide.

This present-day Pied Piper's learned topic was "Health Care: What Is the Value of a Life?" In a nutshell, the value of a life, it seems, is high for him and his liberal elite, but low, that is, *nil*, for the handicapped—the rest of us falling somewhere in between. Singer has also written a book on the blessings of eradicating handicapped children.

None of this has gone unnoticed. In fact, Singer has armed guards when he conducts class to protect him from the rage of those who value life, even the lives, *especially* the lives, of the helpless and suffering. For this, Princeton, that most enlightened of institutions, made Singer a tenured professor at the university's (get this!) Center for Human Values.

Maybe next he'll be awarded the Nobel Prize for his remedy for world suffering, namely, the mercy killing of all "nonviable" specimens.

But haven't we heard all this before, fifty-some years ago? They were called Death Camps for the "misfits." I think some of them still exist in China, Korea, and elsewhere.

Bizarrely, Herr Doktor Singer is the offspring of a Holocaust survivor! Not only that, he has a clean liver: no meat, no leather clothing. He doesn't even smoke or drink. But that mustn't detract us; for Adolf Hitler himself was a vegetarian, a teetotaler, and a nonsmoker. He hated for animals to suffer but had no problem watching his human victims hung by the neck from piano wires on telephone poles. Hitler might be seen as the grandfather of the modern "animal rights" movement! In any case, Singer is in familiar company along with his other vegetarian, animal-rights fanatics—whose mantra is "people bad, animals good."

In an earlier book, Singer argues that the life of a person is not necessarily more valuable than that of an animal! This thinking led to the founding of PETA (People for the Ethical Treatment of Animals). No doubt, this recommends Singer for membership in the Democrats' exclusive New World Order.

No wonder the Consortium of Citizens with Disabilities, an organization for the rights of the handicapped, wrote the following protest letter to the president of Princeton University: "Our view [is] that the dangerous and barbaric views of Peter Singer regarding infants with disabilities has absolutely no place in American society or academia . . . They are bigoted, hateful, and fly in the face of everything our society and our national policy seek for our constituency."

This, after all, is no academic "professorial debate" on the part of the disabled and handicapped. *They fear for their lives.*

In truth, maybe we should all fear for our lives.

Have you had your I.Q. measured lately? I haven't. Or have you run the obstacle course recently, recited numbers backward, looked at inkblots, or multiplied figures without your calculator? Don't! Maybe some of us wouldn't pass Herr Doktor Singer's "normalcy" tests.

I once wrote that late-term abortionists are the reincarnation of Joseph Mengele, the Nazi Angel of Death. I meant it. I think he has now slithered himself into "Kill the Flawed Kids" Singer as well. Does this sound ugly and grotesque? It is. The spirit of Dr. Mengele chooses his hosts with great skill, without reverence for niceties or good taste.

The spirit of Mengele knows well to start at the weakest point and work from there—with Daschle, Singer, Boxer, Feinstein, or any other willing host. From bringing us to destroy the "deformed" at birth, the "accidents" of lust, or the objects of hatred, he fans out until no one is safe and it's too late to turn back. He is the destroyer.

Dr. Singer wrote, "We must balance the tangible harm to which the traditional ethic gives rise—harm to those whose misery is needlessly prolonged." The Nazis killed their handicapped also "to spare them misery."

Granted, there are a handful of pro-life Democrat detractors in the ranks, just as there are Republicans who hold the pro-death position. However, the majority of Republicans go beyond caring for the "little guy" (as the Dems assert). They also care for the "littlest guy"—the unborn child.

BEWARE THE GOVERNMENT-MEDIA COMPLEX

The crimes of the Democrats were not committed alone. Liberal Democats have had the benefit of an accomplice. Actually, many accomplices. In fact, an entire industry who has been, and remains, in collusion with the left.

Never before in American history has there been such a cozy relationship between the government and the media. It is a relationship that transcends left and right, although it is highly skewed to the left. Based upon everything I'm seeing today, I'm deeply concerned about press freedom.

For centuries, the media's primary role has been to be a thorn in the side of the government. In order to keep the government reasonably honest, the media's job is to constantly poke at the policies and actions of the three branches of government. However, when the media become a thorn in the side of the skeptical private citizen, then they become an arm of the government.

That's why I say, "Beware the Government-Media Complex."

Look how these stories are colored.

When Jews in Israel are killed by terrorist acts, the media call them "people." But when a Palestinian is killed, he is called "a Palestinian." What's the difference? Their casualties are given a nationality and an identity by the media. Not so with the Jewish dead. Worse, with the bloodied bodies of innocent Jewish children lying on the ground, the media recited such trash as "One man's terrorist is another man's freedom fighter."

Here at home, when five revolutionary Mexican socialists beat a lone, elderly white male in Los Angeles, they were featured as "heroes of the revolution" in the local San Francisco newspaper. When a mob of homosexuals burned state offices a few years back because one of their platforms was not accepted by a Republican governor, they were called a "collective voice of the oppressed" in the *San Francisco Chronicle* and the *Examiner*.

When the homosexual radicals broke into San Francisco Republican Party headquarters and terrorized workers and destroyed computers, it was implied that these terrorists were "valiant, oppressed voices." When agitators for the homeless riot, when they burn trash cans and break the law, they're held up as "freedom fighters" for the poor by the left-leaning press.

But if one compassionate conservative dares to speak out, he's condemned to the gulag of media silence, the gulag of media exile. This startling bias in the media is more threatening to the pillars of our republic than even the most ardent conservative might believe.

It is *censorship by default* as well.

What do I mean by "censorship by default"? That's where the

commercial interests of the media moguls are so intertwined with government policy as to create an overly friendly image of government officials and their policies. It may not be as clear as a conspiracy to bias the news, but it results in the same form of censorship of dissent.

This bias is not limited to the left. It is largely a product of left-wing bias when it comes to certain social issues such as immigration, affirmative action, and "gay" rights. But the right also biases the news when it wants to shape fiscal issues to its benefit.

I first began my file on the Government-Media Complex several years ago. I noticed an alarming bias, and I knew this could sink the ship of truth. Surely other administrations have had their friends in high media places. Still, there were many voices and many views of dissent that found their way into the national media. But now, we have a growing media blackout of some serious crimes and misdemeanors, all unsolved to the satisfaction of those with critical faculties of reason.

While the old media hacks beat their journalistic bongos to the rhythm of fruit flies dancing on a rotten tomato, a handful of renegade journalists are actually doing their homework, actually chasing the real story, and thinking for themselves instead of requiring a TelePrompTer that tells them what to think. We only know about these events—such as Linda Daschle's conflict of interest as a lobbyist—because the dam of silence was cracked by this rare breed of journalist.

But for the most part, take any major policy issue and you're going to see the official government line reflected by the media elite. Look at some issues: affirmative action; immigration, legal and illegal; the drug epidemic. How often do you hear about these issues?

You hear a constant refrain, for example, about the dangers of tobacco. But how often do you hear about the growing use of marijuana or the heroin epidemic? You do hear about it now and then, but what you hear mostly is about tobacco, tobacco, tobacco, or welfare, the so-called homelessness issue, taxes, and the other favorite issues to beguile us.

Each and every issue as reflected in the old-line news media—that is, the TV network news and the establishment newspapers and magazines—had a parallel reflection of official government policy.

Listen to me carefully.

Hoover Institution historian Robert Conquest said that in the former Soviet Union the press was totally under the control of the state. All editors were members of the Communist Party. Here in the United States of America a frighteningly imbalanced Washington press corps exists. *Eighty-nine percent of these apparatchiks of the DNC recently voted for the Democrat Party.*

Let me repeat, the media are needed by the public to be and remain a thorn in the side of the government in order to keep the government relatively honest. But when the media instead become a thorn in the side of the skeptical private citizen, the media then become an arm of the government.

Is this not worrisome?

Not only are the media in bed with the government, producing headlines that are merely a reflection of the pillow talk, many of the Demoncats and Republicans are shacking up, too. While I highlight the crimes of the Democrats, I am more and more convinced that we have a one-party oligarchy ruling our nation. Call them "Republicrats" or "Demicans" (your choice). Either way, it's a government of the rich, by the special-interest groups, and for the lobbyists.

The Democrats will take us to the land of socialism on a bullet train. The Republicans will take us there on an express train.

When was the last time you heard any one of our leaders conduct a substantive discussion about our borders, language, or culture? Why is so little if anything said about the immigration crisis, spying, lost nuclear secrets, China's takeover of the Panama Canal, the flood of drugs, the homosexualization of our culture, the feminization of our military, the disaster of affirmative action, the assaults against white America by racial gangsters, Gore's gangster attack against Microsoft and the NASDAQ collapse leading to the Dot.Com collapse, the forced suicide of Israel, the lawyer-liaring of our justice system, the pornographing of our homes, Hollywood's violence against children, voter fraud, media monopolies, the attack on Christianity?

In short, the "Republicrats" and "Demicans" have sacked our Constitution, our culture, our religions, and embarrassed the nation. Not a peep from the Republican "leaders."

Again, the last years of the Weimar Republic of pre-Nazi Germany come to mind—where decadence completely permeated a free society. The advisers to Bush must take a stance in these culture wars.

A MESSAGE TO TEN POLITICIANS

I'm writing this final thought for the benefit of ten people in the United States of America, those of you who hold the reins of power. I want to appeal to your greed and the larceny in your heart. I'm gonna say something to you that somebody has not told you in a long time: The pollsters are wrong.

The American people can't take the ambivalence anymore.

They're ready to snap.

I'm not talking about those who watch daytime television. I'm talking about the hard core of America—they're ready to snap. They can't take the pain anymore. They can't take the lies. They can't handle another day of being told nothing can be done to prevent the flood of illegal immigrants—even from terrorist-sponsoring nations.

If a man or a woman were to stand up in this country now, any one of you senators, congressmen, or governors, stand up right now, like General Patton, and defend our borders, our language, and our culture, you could save America. Your act of leadership and courage would take the reins away from a weak presidency.

The only time Bush gets gigantic ratings, which he rides on for months, is when he becomes the real George Bush. When he becomes the conservative Christian that he is, the Texan who knows right from wrong, good from evil; when he talks about an axis of evil (he really meant an arc of evil, but he had a bad script writer that day). He was right on the money, and the American people responded to it. But then he vacillates and goes the other way. Why? His advisers mislead him.

If you stand up and voice support for Israel and put down Yasser Arafat as the gangster/murderer that he is; if you stand up to the Islam-O-Fascists who want to take over this country and the world; if you stand up against the liberals who would hamstring your efforts to close our borders to illegal immigration; and if you arrest the corporate pirates and seize their assets, you will be a great leader.

I don't know who you are. You could be a senator from Nebraska. You could be a governor from Missouri. Doesn't matter. Bill Clinton came out of nowhere, didn't he? I'll concede the fact that he had the backing of the communist Chinese. They backed him way back in the 1990-91 era. And when he almost lost in his own state, they backed him again. He had loads of money.

No matter what the odds are against you, you'll have loads of money, too. That is, if you stand up and defend America against those who would destroy our faith, our families, and our future. Yes, reignite the spirit of America by protecting our borders, language, and culture, and you will be the next voice of the United States.

AFTERWORD

⌒

THE SAVAGE NATION is the story of one man's love affair with the United States. My grandfather Sam, who was the "astronaut" of the family, fled Russia, came to America, and worked for seven years. One by one, with the iron support of Grandma Fannie, he brought over my family, including my father, who was a little boy. I am living Sam's dreams, and I would do anything to protect the freedoms I enjoy.

Freedom of speech.

Freedom of worship.

Freedom of assembly.

Freedom of travel.

Yet I see an enormous erosion of these freedoms. Not just from the government but also from alien forces within our own society. So-called civil liberty groups continue to attack each of these freedoms in the name of freedom. At the same time, a growing international government, the United Nations, continually attempts to override these freedoms.

If the price of liberty is eternal vigilance, then only a *more* Savage Nation will enjoy these liberties.

ABOUT THE AUTHOR

⌒

BY SIZZLING WITH PASSION and succinct genius, Michael Savage soared to become the #1 afternoon drive-time host in the San Francisco Bay Area. Now heard on over three hundred radio stations, the syndicated *Michael Savage Show* is breaking records. From WABC in New York City, to KLIF in Dallas, and KXL in Portland, Oregon, America is tuning in to Michael Savage.

Fitting no stereotype, he attacks oversized bureaucracies and liberal media bias, but champions the environment and animal rights.

Deriving his political views from Plato, Aristotle, and the rugged individualist-affirming literature of earlier times, Savage spikes his delivery with quotes from Plato's *Republic,* Ralph Waldo Emerson's *Self-Reliance,* Gibbon's *History of Rome,* and many other classical works of philosophy.

Passionate about science, Michael Savage is highly educated. He holds one master's degree in medical botany, another in medical anthropology, and earned his Ph.D. from the University of California at Berkeley in epidemiology and nutrition science. He's also an ardent conservationist and dog owner. He brings all his interests into play through active debate with his callers, regardless of their political inclinations.

Along with the book *The Savage Nation* and CD *Best of The*

Savage Nation, he is author of the book *Herbs That Heal* and seventeen other books. He spent many years as an ethno-botanist, collecting medicinal plants throughout many islands of the South Pacific.

Savage first popularized the phrase "Compassionate Conservative" in 1994 and has since used this concept in his radio program and in conducting hugely successful conventions bearing that name. Savage has consistently drawn sold-out audiences to hear him live. For Savage, these words describe a "firewall of balance" that limits how far to the right his opinions go.

"I want to elevate the dialogue, if I can, to some level that's civil," he says. "People are real pent-up. They've been silenced for a long time. My show offers them an outlet, while standing up to the Red-Diaper-Doper-Babies (RDDB) who rule the illiberal establishment."

To learn more about Michael Savage and his efforts to defend America's **borders, language, and culture,** visit **www.MichaelSavage.com.**